AF258422

a very long story nobody asked for

by

Published by **Untold Imprint**

www.sdarling-art.com

ISBN: 978-1-7641672-4-6

Printed in Australia

This work is a collection of philosophical reflections and observations about life, written as a continuous narrative.

The ideas presented are intended to provoke thought and reflection and should not be interpreted as objective truths, professional advice, or factual accounts of specific individuals or events.

Any resemblance to real persons, living or dead is purely coincidental.

Nobody asked for this story.

That's probably the best place to begin.

No one requested it.

No one sat down and said,

"Please explain life to us."

And yet people spend most of their lives searching for explanations.

For meaning.

For answers.

For something that makes all the confusion feel intentional.

The strange part is that many of the answers people spend years searching for…

are usually hiding in places they refuse to look.

Mostly inside themselves.

Which is inconvenient.

Because that's the one place people tend to avoid.

Life is strange that way.

People will travel across the world trying to find themselves.

They will climb mountains.

Attend retreats.

Listen to speakers who promise clarity.

They will read books written by strangers who claim to understand the meaning of existence.

But sitting quietly with their own thoughts for ten minutes?

That is usually where the real discomfort begins.

Silence has a habit of revealing things.

Things people would prefer not to notice.

Questions they've been avoiding.

Doubts they've carefully pushed aside.

And occasionally something even more unsettling.

The realization that many of the things they believed about life…

were never really examined at all.

They were simply accepted.

Passed down like instructions.

Follow these rules.

Make these choices.

Aim for these goals.

And everything will work out the way it's supposed to.

At least that's the idea.

It sounds comforting.

Which is probably why so many people accept it without asking too many questions.

Because questioning the rules of life can be a dangerous exercise.

Once you begin…

it becomes difficult to stop.

Sometimes that realization begins in childhood.

Not in a dramatic way.

There is no announcement.

No moment where someone sits you down and explains it.

It arrives quietly.

Usually through observation.

Children spend years believing that adults understand the world.

It seems obvious.

Adults make decisions.

They set rules.

They explain how things work.

They speak with confidence about what should be done and what should never be done.

From a child's perspective, it all looks very organized.

Almost as if life came with instructions that adults had already learned to follow.

But eventually small cracks begin to appear in that illusion.

Maybe you overhear a conversation you weren't meant to hear.

Two adults discussing something in uncertain voices.

Not explaining the world…

but trying to figure it out themselves.

Maybe you notice hesitation.

A pause before someone answers a question they are supposed to understand.

Or you watch an adult make a decision that clearly doesn't make sense.

At first these moments are confusing.

Children assume adults must have reasons.

Hidden explanations.

Plans that simply haven't been revealed yet.

But the older you become, the harder it is to ignore what you are seeing.

Adults aren't following instructions.

They are improvising.

Just like everyone else.

That realization can be unsettling at first.

If adults don't actually understand everything…

then who does?

For a while that question lingers quietly in the background.

Most people don't ask it directly.

Because the answer isn't particularly comforting.

The truth is that nobody fully understands life.

People simply become more experienced at navigating uncertainty.

They learn patterns.

They learn consequences.

They learn what tends to work and what tends to fail.

But certainty?

That remains surprisingly rare.

Even among the people who appear most confident.

Especially among them.

This is one of the strange transitions between childhood and adulthood.

At some point the world stops feeling like a structured system…

and starts feeling more like a complicated improvisation.

People trying their best.

Sometimes succeeding.

Often guessing.

Occasionally pretending to understand things they secretly don't.

And the strange part is that this realization doesn't immediately make life easier.

If anything, it introduces new questions.

If nobody truly understands everything…

then how are decisions supposed to be made?

How does someone choose the right path?

The right career.

The right partner.

The right life.

Most people assume there must be a clear answer somewhere.

A correct direction.

A hidden formula for getting things right.

But life rarely provides formulas.

It provides choices.

And then waits to see what happens next.

And that is where things start becoming complicated.

Because choices sound simple in theory.

But they rarely feel simple when you are the one making them.

Most decisions arrive without clear instructions.

No guarantees.

No obvious confirmation that you are moving in the right direction.

Just a quiet moment where something inside you says,

This seems like the right thing to do.

So you try.

Sometimes it works.

Sometimes it doesn't.

And often the difference between those two outcomes only becomes clear years later.

One of the strange things about life is that people expect certainty long before certainty becomes possible.

Young people are asked what they want to do with their lives.

Which is an interesting question.

Not because it is unreasonable.

But because it assumes something that rarely exists at that age.

Clarity.

Most people at that stage are still trying to understand themselves.

Their interests.

Their abilities.

Their fears.

The idea that someone should already know the direction of their entire life can feel almost absurd.

And yet the question appears again and again.

At school.

At family gatherings.

In casual conversations.

So what do you want to do with your life?

Many people answer confidently.

Not because they truly know.

But because uncertainty rarely sounds impressive.

Confidence, on the other hand, does.

Confidence suggests direction.

Purpose.

Control.

Three things society tends to admire.

Even when they are only partially true.

The performance begins quietly.

At first it is small.

People start presenting themselves as slightly more certain than they actually feel.

They talk about plans.

Goals. Careers. The future.

Sometimes those plans are genuine.

Sometimes they are simply the best guess available at the time.

But once a plan is spoken out loud, something interesting happens.

It begins to feel real.

Expectations form around it.

Family members encourage It.

Friends assume it will happen.

And gradually the plan transforms into something heavier.

Not just an idea anymore.

But an identity.

This is how many people begin building lives.

Not by discovering a clear path…

but by slowly committing to the direction that seemed reasonable at the time.

Sometimes that direction turns out to be meaningful.

Sometimes it leads somewhere unexpected.

And occasionally it becomes something people quietly outgrow.

The difficult part is that life rarely pauses to ask if the direction still feels right.

Time continues moving.

Responsibilities accumulate.

Decisions build on top of previous decisions.

And before long, what began as a simple choice becomes something much larger.

A career. A reputation. A life structure.

Something that would now be complicated to change.

Not impossible.

But complicated.

Complication is something people rarely talk about when they describe success.

Success stories are usually told in straight lines.

A person decides what they want.

They work hard.

They overcome a few obstacles.

And eventually everything falls into place.

It makes for a very satisfying narrative.

It also leaves out a great deal of reality.

Because most lives do not unfold in straight lines.

They move in circles.

Detours.

Unexpected turns that only make sense much later.

Sometimes not even then.

People often imagine that other lives are more organized than their own.

That somewhere out there are individuals who truly know what they are doing.

People with plans that actually unfold exactly the way they expected.

But if you spend enough time observing others…

that illusion begins to fade.

You notice hesitation.

Changes of direction.

Quiet adjustments that are rarely mentioned out loud.

Careers that evolve.

Dreams that shift.

Plans that are rewritten halfway through.

This is one of the strange discoveries of adulthood.

Everyone appears confident from a distance.

But confidence looks different when you stand close enough to see the details.

You begin to notice that certainty is often just momentum.

People continuing in a direction because they started moving that way long ago.

Not necessarily because they carefully chose it.

At some point you might notice something similar in your own life.

A moment where you stop and look around at the path you have been following.

Not questioning it exactly.

Just observing it.

How did I end up here?

It's not always a dramatic realization.

Sometimes it arrives during very ordinary moments.

Driving somewhere familiar.

Walking home after a long day.

Sitting quietly with a thought that refuses to leave.

And suddenly you notice something that had been there all along.

Life has been unfolding around you while you were busy trying to understand it.

This realization is not necessarily uncomfortable.

In fact, for some people it can be strangely reassuring.

Because once you recognize how uncertain most lives actually are…

the pressure to have everything perfectly figured out begins to loosen.

Not disappear.

But loosen.

People still try, of course.

They continue presenting their lives in confident terms.

Talking about where they are going.

What they are building.

What they intend to become.

And sometimes those descriptions are accurate.

Sometimes they are simply hopeful.

But hope has always been one of the more reliable engines of human behavior.

Without it, very few people would attempt anything ambitious.

Hope makes uncertainty easier to carry.

It allows people to keep moving forward even when the destination is not entirely clear.

Which is fortunate.

Because if everyone waited until they fully understood life before making decisions…

very little would ever happen.

If you think about it long enough, you may notice something interesting.

Many of the decisions that shaped your life probably did not feel monumental at the time.

They felt ordinary.

A job accepted.

A move to a new place.

A conversation that led somewhere unexpected.

A moment where one choice seemed slightly more reasonable than another.

And only years later do those moments reveal their significance.

Life has a habit of disguising important turning points as ordinary days.

Which is why people rarely recognize them while they are happening.

They only become obvious when seen in reverse.

And somewhere along the way another realization begins to appear.

A quieter one.

People start comparing their lives to the lives of others.

Not always intentionally.

Sometimes it happens gradually.

Through small observations.

A friend who seems to be moving ahead.

Someone who appears to have found direction earlier.

Someone who looks as if they understand life better than you do.

At least from the outside.

From a distance, other lives often appear remarkably well organized.

Careers progressing smoothly.

Relationships forming naturally.

Plans unfolding exactly the way they were supposed to.

It can create the impression that everyone else received a map…

and you somehow missed the instructions.

But distance has always been good at hiding complexity.

When you look closely enough at almost any life…

you begin to see the same patterns again.

Uncertainty.

Doubt.

Improvisation.

People making the best decision they can with the information they have at the time.

And hoping it leads somewhere worthwhile.

And that hope carries people surprisingly far.

Far enough that most lives begin to resemble carefully planned
journeys.

At least from the outside.

People appear to move forward with purpose.

Careers develop.

Relationships form.

Homes are built.

Milestones appear one after another.

Graduations.

Promotions.

Weddings.

Announcements about new beginnings.

From a distance it can look as if life follows a very predictable
sequence.

Almost like a schedule.

Step one.

Step two.

Step three.

But life rarely unfolds according to a shared timeline.

That realization usually arrives quietly.

Often through comparison.

Someone you know seems to be progressing faster.

They appear certain.

Focused.

Confident about where they are going.

And suddenly a small question begins forming in the back of the mind.

Not loudly.

Just quietly enough to be uncomfortable.

Am I behind?

It is a strange question.

Because nobody ever clearly explains what the correct timeline is supposed to be.

There is no official schedule for life.

No universal moment when success must appear.

No agreement on when someone should have everything figured out.

And yet the feeling persists.

The sense that progress should look a certain way.

That life should unfold according to an invisible clock.

Comparison makes that clock feel louder.

You notice people reaching milestones.

Buying homes.

Starting families.

Building careers.

Making plans that sound permanent.

And it becomes easy to assume that everyone else has discovered something you have not.

Some secret understanding of how life is supposed to work.

But if you speak honestly with enough people…

another pattern begins to appear.

Behind confident descriptions of success are often the same quiet uncertainties.

People adjusting their plans.

Reconsidering decisions.

Wondering if they chose the right direction.

Sometimes long after the choice has already been made.

The strange part is that these doubts are rarely visible from the outside.

Most people only see the surface of other lives.

The achievements.

The announcements.

The moments that look decisive and intentional.

They rarely see the hesitation that came before them.

Or the uncertainty that sometimes follows afterward.

Which creates one of the more persistent illusions of adulthood.

Everyone appears certain.

Until you begin listening closely enough to hear the hesitation beneath the surface.

Hesitation is something people learn to hide surprisingly well.

Not because they are dishonest.

But because uncertainty rarely fits comfortably into conversation.

When people ask how life is going, they expect simple answers.

Clear direction.

Progress.

Very few conversations begin with someone calmly explaining that they are still figuring everything out.

Even though that is usually the truth.

So people describe their lives in confident language.

They talk about where they are heading.

What they are building.

What they plan to become.

And often those descriptions are sincere.

But sincerity does not always mean certainty.

Sometimes it simply means commitment.

A decision made long enough ago that it now feels permanent.

Momentum has a way of turning decisions into identities.

At first a choice is just a direction.

A job accepted.

A field of study.

A place to live.

But as time passes, the choice becomes something more substantial.

People begin introducing themselves through it.

This is what I do.

This is where I belong.

This is the life I am building.

And for a while that identity feels stable.

Comforting, even.

It gives life a sense of structure.

A story that makes sense when told out loud.

But structure has a subtle side effect.

Once a direction becomes part of someone's identity…

changing it begins to feel more difficult than choosing it in the first place.

Because changing direction does not only affect the future.

It also rewrites the past.

Suddenly years of effort need to be reconsidered.

Plans that once felt logical begin to look uncertain.

People start asking questions.

What happened?

Why the change?

And explaining those decisions can feel surprisingly complicated.

Even when the answer is simple.

Sometimes the answer is simply this.

People grow.

What felt right at one moment in life may not feel the same years later.

Interests evolve.

Values shift.

Priorities rearrange themselves quietly over time.

But momentum does not always adjust as easily as people do.

So many individuals continue moving forward long after the original reason for choosing that direction has faded.

Not because they are trapped.

But because movement itself becomes familiar.

And familiarity can be a powerful force.

At some point, however, most people experience a quiet moment of reflection.

A pause long enough to ask a simple question.

If I were starting again today…

would I choose this same path?

The answer is not always clear.

And that uncertainty can be uncomfortable.

But it also reveals something important.

Life is not a single decision made once.

It is a series of decisions that quietly reshape themselves over time.

Sometimes intentionally.

Sometimes simply because people continue moving forward.

And movement can be deceptive.

When people are moving, it feels as if progress is happening.

Direction creates a sense of purpose.

Plans create a sense of control.

Even when the destination remains unclear.

So many individuals continue moving forward without stopping long enough to ask whether the path still belongs to them.

Because stopping introduces a different kind of uncertainty.

And uncertainty has a way of making people uncomfortable.

It is often easier to continue than to reconsider.

Continuing requires effort.

But reconsidering requires honesty.

And honesty can be far more demanding.

To reconsider something honestly means admitting that the original decision might no longer fit the person you have become.

That realization can feel unsettling.

Especially when the decision has shaped years of your life.

For that reason, many people become skilled at explaining their choices to themselves.

They create reasonable arguments.

Practical explanations.

Convincing narratives about why continuing forward is the correct thing to do.

Sometimes those explanations are accurate.

Sometimes they are simply comforting.

But comfort has always been persuasive.

There is nothing unusual about this.

Human beings are remarkably good at adapting to circumstances.

They learn routines.

They grow familiar with environments.

They build lives around the structures that already exist.

And once something becomes familiar, leaving it behind begins to feel more difficult than remaining.

Even when remaining quietly produces dissatisfaction.

This is why so many people discover something interesting about comfort.

Comfort is not always the same thing as happiness.

Sometimes it is simply the absence of change.

The familiarity of what already exists.

And familiarity has a way of making even imperfect situations feel acceptable.

At least for a while.

But time has a way of gradually revealing whether a direction truly fits.

People begin noticing small signals.

Restlessness.

A quiet curiosity about other possibilities.

The sense that something important might still be waiting somewhere beyond the life they currently understand.

At first these thoughts appear only occasionally.

They arrive during quiet moments.

Late at night.

On long walks.

During conversations that unexpectedly drift into deeper territory.

Most of the time they pass quickly.

Life continues.

Responsibilities return.

The familiar structure of daily routine takes over again.

But some questions have a habit of returning.

Not loudly.

Just persistently.

And each time they return, they become a little more difficult to ignore.

One of those questions is surprisingly simple.

Is this the life I truly want to live?

For some people the answer arrives immediately.

For others it remains uncertain for years.

But the moment the question appears, something changes.

Because once a question like that exists…

the possibility of a different life begins to exist alongside it.

And possibilities can be unsettling things.

Not because they are dangerous.

But because they introduce alternatives.

Once people realize that another path might exist, the current one begins to look different.

What once felt permanent starts to feel optional.

What once felt inevitable starts to feel chosen.

And choices, once recognized, become difficult to ignore.

For many people this is where hesitation begins.

Not because they lack courage.

But because they recognize the weight of what has already been built.

Years invested in a direction.

Effort spent learning a profession.

Relationships formed around a certain version of themselves.

Changing direction does not only affect the future.

It forces someone to reconsider the past.

There is a quiet fear hidden in that realization.

The fear that starting again might mean admitting that earlier choices were wrong.

But life rarely works that way.

Most decisions are not mistakes.

They are simply steps taken with the understanding available at the time.

People choose what seems reasonable.

What seems promising.

What seems possible.

And only later do they discover where those choices actually lead.

The difficulty comes from something psychologists sometimes call investment.

The more time and energy people invest in something, the harder
it becomes to walk away from it.

Even when they quietly suspect that the direction may no longer
be right.

Because leaving can feel like losing what has already been spent.

Years.

Effort.

Identity.

But time has an interesting characteristic.

It moves forward regardless of whether people reconsider their
direction or not.

Which means that staying somewhere purely because of time
already invested does not actually preserve that time.

It simply adds more of it.

That realization can be uncomfortable.

But it also introduces a different perspective.

Life is not a contract signed once and followed forever.

It is something that continues unfolding as long as a person is
willing to participate in it.

And participation sometimes means adjusting direction.

Not dramatically.

Sometimes only slightly.

But enough to acknowledge that people change.

The strange part is that many individuals quietly admire those who make such changes.

The person who begins a new career later in life.

The individual who moves somewhere unfamiliar.

Someone who decides to pursue something that once felt unrealistic.

From the outside, these decisions often look courageous.

From the inside, they usually begin with a much simpler feeling.

A quiet recognition that something else might be possible.

And possibility, once recognized, tends to remain.

Even when ignored for a while.

Possibility has a quiet persistence.

It does not always demand attention.

Most of the time it waits patiently in the background.

Life continues.

Work continues.

Responsibilities continue.

Days pass with the familiar rhythm of routine.

And yet, somewhere beneath all of that movement, the awareness remains.

Something else might exist.

Another direction.

Another version of life that has not yet been explored.

What makes this realization interesting is that people rarely lack imagination.

Most individuals are capable of envisioning very different lives for themselves.

They can imagine living somewhere new.

Learning something unfamiliar.

Becoming someone slightly different from the person they have been so far.

The imagination allows those possibilities to appear clearly.

But imagination alone rarely produces change.

Because imagining a different life is easy.

Living it is much more complicated.

Not because the idea itself is difficult.

But because life is rarely lived in isolation.

Every person exists inside a network of expectations.

Family.

Friends.

Colleagues.

Communities that quietly form around the identity someone has already created.

And identities tend to come with assumptions.

People expect continuity.

They expect the person they know today to resemble the person they knew yesterday.

Which is usually reasonable.

Consistency makes relationships easier to understand.

But it also creates an invisible pressure.

The pressure to remain recognizable.

To continue being the version of yourself that others have already accepted.

Most of the time this pressure is subtle.

No one announces it directly.

No one gathers in a room and demands that someone remain exactly the same.

Instead it appears through smaller signals.

Surprise when someone changes direction.

Questions about why something different is suddenly necessary.

Comments that gently suggest returning to what is familiar.

None of these reactions are unusual.

They come from a natural human instinct.

People prefer stability.

They prefer knowing where things are going.

Uncertainty can make even supportive individuals uncomfortable.

So when someone begins considering a different path, the responses they receive are often cautious.

Not discouraging exactly.

But careful.

Measured.

Concerned.

Which can make change feel far larger than it actually is.

Because now the decision does not only affect the person making it.

It also affects how others understand them.

And human beings are social creatures.

We tend to care deeply about how we are perceived by the people around us.

This is why courage often looks easier from a distance.

Watching someone else take a risk can feel inspiring.

Admirable.

Even obvious.

Of course they should follow what feels right.

Of course they should try something new.

But standing inside the decision feels very different.

From that position, the unknown becomes much more visible.

And uncertainty has always been one of the most powerful forces shaping human behavior.

Not because people dislike possibility.

But because possibility is inseparable from risk.

Every new direction carries the potential for failure.

For disappointment.

For discovering that the imagined future does not unfold the way it was hoped.

So people hesitate.

Not forever.

But long enough to weigh the cost of change against the comfort of familiarity.

And in many cases, familiarity wins.

Not because it is perfect.

But because it is known.

The known has a certain comfort to it.

Even when it isn't particularly satisfying.

People grow familiar with routines.

Predictable environments.

The small patterns that quietly shape everyday life.

Wake up.

Work.

Return home.

Repeat.

There is something reassuring about knowing what tomorrow will look like.

Familiarity makes the world feel stable.

Even if that stability sometimes hides a quiet sense that something might be missing.

For that reason many people develop an interesting habit.

They begin waiting.

Not necessarily waiting for something specific.

Just waiting for the right moment.

The right opportunity.

The right circumstances that will somehow make change feel easier.

The idea seems sensible.

If the conditions improve, then action will feel more natural.

If the timing is better, decisions will become clearer.

If the situation aligns perfectly, the next step will reveal itself.

But life rarely arranges itself with that level of precision.

The moment people imagine the perfect moment has a curious tendency to remain just out of reach.

There is always something that suggests waiting a little longer.

A responsibility that should probably be handled first.

A situation that needs to stabilize.

A detail that should be clarified before making any significant move.

Each reason seems reasonable.

And individually, they often are.

But together they can create a quiet delay that stretches far longer than expected.

Years pass this way for many people.

Not because they lack intention.

But because they are waiting for clarity that life rarely provides in advance.

Clarity usually arrives in a different form.

It arrives after action.

After movement.

After someone takes a step without knowing exactly how everything will unfold.

That idea can feel uncomfortable.

Because people prefer certainty before commitment.

It feels safer.

More responsible.

But certainty is a rare luxury in life.

Most meaningful decisions happen long before certainty appears.

This is why courage is often misunderstood.

Courage is not the absence of doubt.

It is movement in spite of it.

People who make significant changes in their lives rarely feel completely prepared.

They simply reach a point where remaining still begins to feel more uncomfortable than moving forward.

And that moment, when it arrives, tends to be surprisingly quiet.

There is rarely a dramatic announcement.

No sudden clarity that explains every consequence.

Just a simple recognition.

Perhaps it is time to try something different.

That realization can feel larger than it actually is.

Because once someone begins considering a different direction, another thought often appears alongside it.

What will people think?

It is a remarkably common concern.

Not because people are unusually insecure.

But because human beings are deeply social.

For most of history survival depended on belonging to a group.

Acceptance mattered.

Reputation mattered.

Being understood by others mattered.

Those instincts have not disappeared simply because modern life looks different.

So when someone considers making a change, the reactions of others can begin to feel very important.

Family members may have expectations.

Friends may have assumptions.

Colleagues may have formed ideas about who you are and what your life represents.

Changing direction can feel as if it might disrupt those expectations.

And the possibility of that disruption can make hesitation feel reasonable.

But something interesting often becomes clear with time.

Most people are far more focused on their own lives than we imagine.

They have their own questions.

Their own uncertainties.

Their own quiet decisions they are trying to make sense of.

Which means that the amount of attention people believe they are receiving is often greatly exaggerated.

This realization can be strangely freeing.

Not because other people stop caring entirely.

But because their attention tends to move quickly.

Today's surprising decision becomes tomorrow's normal reality.

People adjust.

They adapt.

They continue with their own lives.

What once felt like a dramatic shift slowly becomes part of the background.

The same way many past decisions eventually became ordinary.

A new city becomes home.

A different profession becomes routine.

A new version of life gradually replaces the one that existed before.

And the world continues turning without much disruption at all.

This is one of the quiet truths about human perception.

We imagine that our lives are being observed far more closely than they actually are.

In reality, most people are busy navigating their own stories.

Their own uncertainties.

Their own attempts to understand how life is unfolding around them.

Once someone begins to recognize this, a certain kind of freedom appears.

The freedom to experiment.

The freedom to change direction.

The freedom to admit that life is still being discovered rather than perfectly planned.

And that freedom can make the future feel a little less intimidating.

Not because uncertainty disappears.

But because uncertainty becomes something shared.

Everyone is navigating it in their own way.

Some people simply hide it more convincingly than others.

Which means the confidence people observe in others is often a performance.

Not an intentional deception.

Just a habit.

People learn to present their lives as organized.

Directed.

Purposeful.

Because that version of life is easier to explain.

And easier for others to understand.

Uncertainty, on the other hand, is difficult to summarize.

It rarely fits comfortably into conversation.

When someone asks how things are going, the expected response is simple.

Good.

Busy.

Moving forward.

Very few people answer honestly enough to say that they are still trying to understand what direction their life should take.

Even though that is often the truth.

So people describe the version of life that sounds most coherent.

Plans.

Ambitions.

Goals that appear clear and intentional.

Sometimes those descriptions are accurate.

Sometimes they are simply the best story available at the moment.

A way of organizing the uncertainty into something that feels manageable.

This is how many lives begin to resemble carefully written narratives.

Stories about where someone started.

Where they are going.

What they intend to become.

And stories are powerful things.

Once repeated often enough, they begin to feel real.

Even when the person telling the story quietly wonders whether the direction still feels right.

There is nothing unusual about this.

Human beings have always used stories to understand their lives.

We organize experiences into meaning.

We explain past decisions in ways that make them appear logical.

And we describe the future as if it is unfolding according to a plan.

Because the alternative is harder to describe.

The alternative is simply life unfolding moment by moment.

Without a clear script.

Without certainty.

For a while this narrative works well.

It creates structure.

Direction.

A sense that life is progressing toward something understandable.

But occasionally the story begins to feel less convincing.

Not because it is completely wrong.

But because something inside the person telling it begins to change.

Values evolve.

Interests shift.

Priorities rearrange themselves in ways that were difficult to imagine earlier in life.

And slowly the narrative that once explained everything begins to feel incomplete.

This is usually when people begin asking deeper questions.

Not about what they should achieve next.

But about why they wanted certain things in the first place.

That question can be surprisingly difficult to answer.

Because many of the goals people pursue feel so natural that they rarely stop to examine where those goals originated.

Success.

Stability.

Recognition.

Security.

These ideas appear so frequently in conversation that they begin to feel universal.

Almost as if everyone naturally wants the same things.

But the origins of those ambitions are often more complicated.

Some come from family expectations.

Ideas about what a respectable life should look like.

Advice offered by people who genuinely want the best for someone, even if their definition of "best" was shaped by a very different time.

Other ambitions come from observation.

Watching what appears to work for others.

Seeing which paths seem to produce admiration.

Which careers attract respect.

Which lifestyles appear comfortable from the outside.

Over time those observations quietly form a map of what a successful life is supposed to resemble.

And maps can be useful.

They provide direction.

They help people avoid obvious mistakes.

But maps are always drawn from someone else's perspective.

They describe the terrain as it appeared to the person who created them.

Not necessarily the person who is now following them.

So many people spend years traveling along routes they inherited rather than consciously chose.

Not because the direction is wrong.

But because it was accepted long before anyone asked whether it truly belonged to them.

Eventually the question returns.

Not urgently.

Just persistently enough to deserve attention.

Is this something I genuinely want?

Or is it simply something I learned to want?

That distinction can feel subtle at first.

But once someone begins noticing it, their understanding of life changes.

Ambition begins to look different.

Success begins to look different.

Even the idea of progress begins to shift.

Because progress toward something that was never deeply desired can begin to feel strangely empty.

Not immediately.

Sometimes it takes years to recognize.

But the absence of meaning eventually becomes difficult to ignore.

Which is why some of the most thoughtful moments in adulthood arrive unexpectedly.

Not when someone achieves something impressive.

But when they pause long enough to reconsider what they are actually pursuing.

Because achievement has an interesting effect on people.

For years it exists in the distance.

Something imagined.

Something pursued with determination.

It becomes a symbol of what life will eventually feel like once the effort has paid off.

Clarity.

Satisfaction.

A sense that everything finally makes sense.

People often describe these moments as arrival.

The point where all the previous effort leads somewhere meaningful.

Where the long climb finally reaches the summit.

And for a brief time that feeling can be real.

Relief appears.

Recognition appears.

The quiet satisfaction of seeing years of work produce visible results.

But something else often follows shortly afterward.

Something far less discussed.

The realization that life does not stop moving once a goal has been reached.

The questions that existed before achievement rarely disappear.

They simply change shape.

People still wake up with the same thoughts.

The same curiosity about what comes next.

The same awareness that life is still unfolding around them.

Even after something significant has been accomplished.

For some individuals this realization arrives quickly.

They reach a goal they spent years pursuing.

And shortly afterward they notice something surprising.

The feeling they expected to last forever quietly fades.

What once felt extraordinary begins to feel normal.

Just another part of life.

At first this can feel confusing.

Because it seems to contradict everything they believed while working toward that goal.

They imagined that reaching it would answer deeper questions.

That it would somehow confirm that their life was now moving in the correct direction.

But achievement rarely provides that kind of certainty.

It provides results.

Circumstances.

Opportunities that did not exist before.

But the deeper experience of living remains remarkably similar.

This does not mean achievement is meaningless.

Far from it.

Ambition has built extraordinary things in the world.

Cities.

Art.

Scientific discoveries.

Entire fields of knowledge that would not exist without people striving toward difficult goals.

But ambition often promises something it cannot fully deliver.

It promises completion.

The feeling that once something is achieved, the search will finally be over.

And life rarely works that way.

Because the moment one summit is reached, the landscape changes.

New possibilities appear. New questions appear.

And the person who reached that summit is no longer the same person who began the climb.

The destination often changes the traveler more than the traveler changes the destination.

Years of effort shape people.

They develop new skills.

New perspectives.

New ways of understanding the world.

And sometimes, by the time they reach the place they once believed would satisfy them completely, they realize they have become someone slightly different from the person who first imagined that goal.

What once felt like the perfect destination now looks different through new eyes.

Not wrong.

Just incomplete.

As if the goal belonged to an earlier version of themselves.

A person who understood life in simpler terms.

This realization does not diminish the effort that led there.

Every path teaches something valuable.

Even the ones that eventually lead somewhere unexpected.

But it does reveal something important about the nature of progress.

Progress is rarely a straight movement toward a permanent conclusion.

It is more like a series of discoveries.

Each step revealing a little more of the landscape.

Each achievement opening a view that was not visible before.

And when that new view appears, people often notice something interesting.

The horizon has moved.

What once looked like the end of the journey now appears to be another beginning.

Another question.

Another direction that might be worth exploring.

At first this can feel frustrating.

People like the idea of completion.

They like the thought that one day everything will finally make sense.

That life will settle into a clear and satisfying form.

But the longer someone observes the world, the more they begin to notice that life rarely settles in that way.

Instead it continues unfolding.

Quietly.

Persistently.

One experience leading to another.

One understanding slowly replacing the last.

This does not mean life lacks meaning.

If anything, it suggests the opposite.

Meaning does not exist at the end of the journey.

It exists within the movement itself.

Within the experience of living long enough to see how perspectives evolve.

And perhaps that is why the idea of arrival can sometimes feel misleading.

Because life rarely behaves like a destination.

It behaves more like a landscape.

Something that reveals itself gradually as people move through it.

Some people spend years searching for the place where everything will finally feel complete.

But eventually many begin to suspect something different.

Perhaps life was never meant to arrive anywhere at all.

People still continue searching for destinations, of course.

It seems to be part of human nature.

The mind likes conclusions.

Clear endings.

Moments where effort produces something final and satisfying.

So even after realizing that life rarely behaves like a finished story, people continue imagining that somewhere ahead there must still be a place where everything finally settles.

A point where the questions stop.

Where uncertainty fades.

Where the path that once felt confusing suddenly reveals its purpose.

This idea is comforting.

It suggests that the long process of trying to understand life will eventually lead somewhere clear.

Somewhere stable.

A place where the effort of searching will finally feel justified.

And sometimes life does offer moments that resemble arrival.

A long-pursued goal is achieved.

A difficult chapter of life ends.

A new beginning appears that feels meaningful and promising.

For a while these moments can feel like conclusions.

Like the final page of a long story.

But stories have a habit of continuing.

The mind adjusts to new circumstances surprisingly quickly.

What once felt extraordinary becomes familiar.

What once felt like a destination slowly turns into another starting point.

Which is why so many people eventually notice something interesting about success.

It rarely feels the way they imagined it would while they were pursuing it.

The excitement fades.

The novelty settles.

And life quietly resumes its ordinary rhythm.

Morning arrives.

Work continues.

New problems appear.

New decisions ask to be made.

And the person who once believed they were approaching a final destination suddenly finds themselves standing at the beginning of another journey.

This does not mean the earlier pursuit was meaningless.

Every effort shapes the person making it.

Every challenge builds understanding.

But it does reveal something important about the nature of human ambition.

Ambition is rarely satisfied by arrival.

It is sustained by movement.

People climb mountains for many reasons.

Achievement.

Recognition.

Curiosity.

But if you listen closely to those who climb the most difficult mountains, they often admit something unexpected.

The summit is rarely the most meaningful part.

It is the climb that changes them.

The effort.

The difficulty.

The long moments of uncertainty where continuing requires something deeper than motivation.

Something closer to persistence.

Which is perhaps why human beings keep searching for new horizons.

Not because they truly expect life to end at the top of the next mountain.

But because movement itself reveals something about who they are becoming.

And becoming is one of the quieter aspects of life.

It rarely announces itself.

There is no moment where someone clearly notices the exact point where they changed.

Growth tends to happen gradually.

Through experiences that seem ordinary while they are happening.

Through decisions that only reveal their importance years later.

People often imagine that personal change arrives through dramatic events.

A breakthrough.

A sudden realization.

A moment that divides life into before and after.

And sometimes those moments do occur.

But more often change happens through something much less visible.

Time.

Time introduces people to versions of themselves they had never previously considered.

A younger person imagines the future with certain assumptions.

Certain ambitions.

Certain expectations about what life should eventually become.

But as the years pass, those assumptions begin to evolve.

Not all at once.

Just slowly enough that the change feels natural.

The things that once seemed essential begin to feel optional.

Other things that once seemed unimportant gradually reveal their value.

Time rearranges priorities in ways that are difficult to anticipate.

Which is perhaps why people sometimes look back at earlier versions of themselves with a quiet sense of curiosity.

Not regret.

Just curiosity.

They remember what they once believed life was supposed to be.

And they notice how different their understanding has become.

The ambitions that once felt urgent may now feel distant.

The worries that once seemed overwhelming may now appear smaller than they once did.

And experiences that once felt ordinary may now appear more meaningful in retrospect.

This is one of the subtle gifts of perspective.

Life rarely explains itself while it is happening.

Meaning tends to appear afterward.

Slowly.

As people gather enough experiences to recognize the patterns that were invisible at the time.

And once those patterns begin to appear, the idea of arrival begins to look even more uncertain.

Because the person who eventually arrives somewhere is never the same person who first imagined that destination.

This is one of the quieter paradoxes of life.

People spend years trying to plan the future with precision.

They imagine what the coming years should look like.

Where they will live.

What they will build.

Who they will become.

And there is nothing unreasonable about that effort.

Planning creates direction.

It gives people a sense that life is moving toward something intentional.

But the longer someone observes life, the more they begin to notice something curious.

Many of the most important moments were never part of the plan.

The conversation that changed a relationship.

The unexpected opportunity that altered a career.

The difficult experience that quietly reshaped how someone understood the world.

These moments rarely announce themselves in advance.

They arrive quietly.

Often disguised as ordinary days.

A phone call. A chance meeting.

A decision that seemed small at the time.

Only later do people recognize how much those moments influenced everything that followed.

This realization can be unsettling at first.

Because it challenges the comforting idea that life can be fully organized.

That careful planning will protect people from uncertainty.

But uncertainty has always been part of the landscape.

It exists whether people acknowledge it or not.

Over time many individuals begin to develop a different relationship with this uncertainty.

Instead of trying to eliminate it completely, they learn to live alongside it.

Plans still exist.

Goals still exist.

But they begin to feel slightly more flexible.

Less like rigid instructions.

More like directions that may evolve as new experiences appear.

And with that shift, something interesting happens.

The pressure to control every detail of life begins to loosen.

Not disappear entirely.

But loosen enough that people start paying closer attention to the experiences unfolding around them.

Because life is rarely happening only in the future.

It is happening constantly in the present.

In conversations.

In small decisions.

In quiet moments that might not seem significant until much later.

The future may still matter.

But it slowly stops feeling like the only place where meaning exists.

For many people this realization arrives gradually.

Not through a single moment.

But through a quiet accumulation of experiences.

Years spent preparing for the life they imagined was waiting somewhere ahead.

Studying.

Working.

Building something that would eventually allow them to begin living the way they intended.

At first this approach feels sensible.

Preparation seems responsible.

It suggests patience.

Discipline.

A willingness to delay immediate comfort for something greater later on.

And in many cases that patience produces real benefits.

Skills develop.

Opportunities expand.

Life becomes more stable than it once was.

But occasionally people begin to notice something unexpected.

The life they were preparing for never fully arrives.

Because the preparation itself quietly becomes life.

The years spent building the future were never separate from living.

They were living.

This realization can feel surprising.

Many individuals spent so long imagining that real life would begin later that they did not fully recognize the years that were already unfolding.

Friendships that formed along the way.

Moments of laughter.

Moments of difficulty.

Experiences that shaped them long before the future they imagined ever appeared.

It is only in hindsight that these moments reveal their significance.

People look back and notice that the years they once described as "the beginning" were actually rich with experiences they did not fully appreciate at the time.

This is one of the peculiar aspects of anticipation.

When people focus too intensely on what lies ahead, the present can begin to feel like a waiting room.

A temporary space.

A place where life is simply preparing itself to begin.

But life rarely behaves that way.

It does not pause politely while people make plans.

It continues unfolding regardless of whether they are paying attention to it or not.

Which means that the moments people once believed were only preparation were often the very moments that shaped who they eventually became.

And this is where another quiet realization often appears.

Many of the things people spend years pursuing are not actually about the things themselves.

They are about the feelings those things are expected to produce.

Security. Recognition. Peace of mind.

The sense that life is finally under control.

The goal becomes a symbol.

A way of imagining how life might feel once something important has been achieved.

A certain career promises stability.

A certain level of success promises freedom.

A certain version of life promises happiness.

And because those feelings are deeply appealing, the goals associated with them become powerful motivators.

There is nothing wrong with that instinct.

Human beings naturally move toward experiences that seem meaningful or fulfilling.

But the connection between goals and feelings is not always as direct as people imagine.

Sometimes the achievement arrives…

but the feeling they expected remains surprisingly distant.

This can be confusing at first.

Someone may accomplish something they spent years working toward.

A milestone that once seemed extremely important.

And yet the emotional change they expected feels smaller than imagined.

Life continues.

Responsibilities continue.

The mind continues asking questions about what comes next.

Over time many people begin to understand something subtle about satisfaction.

It rarely appears exactly where they expected to find it.

Instead it appears in places that were never carefully planned.

In relationships that grew naturally over time.

In moments of curiosity.

In work that feels meaningful for reasons that are difficult to explain.

Meaning has a tendency to emerge rather than obey instructions.

It does not always follow the paths people carefully design.

Sometimes it appears through exploration.

Through trying something unfamiliar.

Through experiences that were never originally part of the plan.

Which is perhaps why some of the most meaningful lives appear unconventional from the outside.

They do not always follow the predictable sequence people imagine success should resemble.

Instead they evolve gradually.

Through curiosity.

Through adjustment.

Through a willingness to notice what feels genuinely alive rather than what merely looks impressive.

Curiosity is an interesting force.

Unlike ambition, it rarely begins with a clear destination.

It starts with a question.

A quiet interest in understanding something more deeply.

A willingness to explore without fully knowing what the outcome might be.

But as people grow older, curiosity is sometimes replaced with something more structured.

Expectations.

Plans.

Practical considerations about what life should look like.

Questions gradually become answers.

Exploration gradually becomes direction.

And curiosity, while never completely disappearing, often becomes quieter.

Yet it has a way of returning.

Often later in life.

Sometimes after people have followed carefully constructed plans for many years.

They begin to notice that the moments that feel most alive are not always the ones connected to achievement.

They are the moments connected to interest.

Engagement.

The experience of discovering something new.

Curiosity invites people into life rather than toward a finish line.

It encourages movement without requiring certainty.

A person follows an interest simply because it feels worth exploring.

And along the way unexpected things begin to appear.

Skills.

Ideas.

Relationships that would never have existed without that initial curiosity.

This is one of the reasons some of the most meaningful paths appear accidental.

From the outside they can look unusual.

A series of decisions that do not follow the conventional map of success.

But from the inside they often feel surprisingly coherent.

Each step leading naturally to the next question.

The next interest.

The next experience worth exploring.

And eventually people begin to recognize something subtle.

Meaning was never hiding at the end of the journey.

It was appearing continuously along the way.

Often in the places they were curious enough to look.

Once people begin to notice this, their relationship with life often changes in subtle ways.

The urge to control every detail begins to soften.

Not because planning becomes meaningless.

Planning can still be useful.

It creates direction.

It helps people organize their efforts.

But the belief that life can be fully controlled begins to lose its hold.

Control promises certainty.

It suggests that if someone plans carefully enough, works hard enough, and avoids enough mistakes, life will unfold exactly the way they intend.

For a long time that belief feels convincing.

It encourages discipline.

Responsibility.

The idea that the future can be shaped through effort alone.

And effort does matter.

Human progress is built on effort.

People build homes.

Communities.

Entire civilizations through careful work and determination.

But life itself remains less predictable than the systems people create within it.

Unexpected things continue to happen.

Opportunities appear where they were never planned.

Difficulties arise without warning.

Moments of significance occur in places that once seemed unimportant.

Gradually people begin to understand that living well may require something slightly different from control.

It requires participation.

Participation means remaining present enough to notice what life is offering.

It means responding to circumstances rather than trying to force them into a rigid structure.

It means recognizing that plans can guide life without needing to imprison it.

This perspective does not eliminate uncertainty.

But it changes how uncertainty feels.

Instead of appearing as a constant threat, it begins to resemble an open landscape.

A space where new experiences may appear.

Where understanding can evolve.

Where life can continue revealing itself in ways no plan could have predicted.

Some people discover this early.

Others only recognize it after many years spent trying to force life into a predictable pattern.

But once the realization appears, it tends to remain.

Because participation feels different from control.

It feels more alive.

Over time many people begin to notice something unexpected about certainty.

For years they believed it was the thing they were searching for.

The moment when all the questions would finally disappear.

When life would feel organized enough to stop wondering what comes next.

But certainty rarely arrives in that form.

Even the most experienced people continue encountering situations they cannot fully predict.

Life remains too complex.

Too varied.

Too filled with unexpected turns to allow complete certainty about anything.

And slowly a different kind of understanding begins to replace the search for absolute answers.

People become less concerned with knowing everything in advance.

They become more interested in recognizing patterns.

Understanding how situations tend to unfold.

Learning how human behavior works.

Learning how their own mind works.

This kind of understanding feels quieter than certainty.

It does not promise perfect control.

Instead it provides perspective.

The ability to recognize familiar situations even when the details are new.

Someone who has lived long enough begins to notice certain patterns repeating themselves.

Ambition rising and falling.

Relationships forming and dissolving.

Moments of difficulty giving way to moments of clarity.

The same questions appearing again and again in different forms.

And through observing these patterns something changes.

Life begins to feel less like a puzzle that must be solved…

and more like an experience that gradually reveals itself.

This shift is subtle.

It does not eliminate questions.

If anything, it often introduces deeper ones.

But the pressure to answer everything immediately begins to fade.

Because people start to understand that some questions exist simply to be lived with.

And strangely enough, that realization can feel more peaceful than certainty ever did.

Because the search for certainty can be exhausting.

It encourages people to believe that life must eventually become perfectly clear.

That one day they will finally understand everything that matters.

Why things happened the way they did.

Where their path is ultimately leading.

What the future is supposed to look like.

But life rarely provides that level of explanation.

Events occur.

Experiences accumulate.

And understanding tends to appear gradually rather than all at once.

Often years after the moments themselves have passed.

This is why people sometimes look back at earlier chapters of their lives with a quiet sense of recognition.

Situations that once felt confusing begin to make more sense.

Difficult periods reveal lessons that were invisible at the time.

Decisions that once seemed uncertain reveal their consequences more clearly with distance.

Perspective has a way of arriving slowly.

Not through sudden certainty.

But through the accumulation of experience.

The gradual realization that life cannot be mastered in the way people once imagined.

And for many individuals this realization changes something important.

They stop trying to control life completely.

They stop trying to predict every outcome.

Instead they begin paying closer attention.

Observing.

Learning.

Allowing life to teach them what it will.

The ambition to master life slowly transforms into something quieter.

A desire to understand it.

And understanding, unlike certainty, does not require final answers.

It only requires patience.

The willingness to keep noticing what life is revealing over time.

Eventually many people discover that the questions they once believed needed immediate answers were never meant to be solved quickly.

They were meant to be lived.

Which may be why the most thoughtful individuals often become calmer as the years pass.

Not because life becomes simpler.

But because they no longer expect it to.

And somewhere along the way they realize something simple.

Life was never asking to be solved.

Only to be understood.

And yet even the calmest understanding of life eventually encounters something that refuses to remain simple.

Other people.

Life can be confusing on its own.

But it becomes far more complicated the moment another person enters the picture.

Because people do not arrive in our lives as blank pages.

They arrive carrying histories.

Memories.

Expectations they may not even realize they have.

And when two different histories meet, something interesting begins to happen.

Life becomes less theoretical.

And far more personal.

For a long time many people assume that relationships are supposed to feel natural.

Effortless.

Two individuals meet.

They recognize something familiar in each other.

Understanding appears almost immediately.

At least that is the version of love most stories prefer to describe.

But reality tends to be more complicated than stories.

Because every person carries a private world that no one else can fully see.

Old experiences.

Old disappointments.

Old ways of protecting themselves from being hurt again.

None of these things appear during the first moments of connection.

They reveal themselves slowly.

Usually through situations that seem very ordinary at first.

A disagreement.

A misunderstanding.

A reaction that feels slightly stronger than expected.

These moments rarely mean that something is broken.

More often they simply reveal the deeper layers of two lives beginning to interact.

And this is where relationships become truly interesting.

Because the closer two people become, the more they begin encountering parts of themselves that had previously remained invisible.

Patience that was never tested before.

Insecurities that quietly existed beneath the surface.

Expectations about love that were never fully examined.

For some individuals this discovery feels uncomfortable.

They believed they were entering a relationship to understand another person.

Only to discover that they are also being asked to understand themselves.

At first this realization can be surprising.

Most people assume that they know themselves reasonably well.

They understand their opinions.

Their preferences.

Their values.

But relationships have a way of introducing situations that were
never previously encountered.

And new situations tend to reveal new parts of a person.

Someone who believed they were patient
may discover how quickly that patience disappears.

Someone who believed they were independent may discover a
quiet desire for reassurance.

Someone who believed they were easy going may suddenly notice
how strongly they react when something important feels
misunderstood.

This is one of the reasons connection can feel so powerful.

It does not simply bring two people together.

It expands self-awareness.

Sometimes gently.

Sometimes unexpectedly.

But almost always in ways that reveal something new.

And yet there is another subtle force shaping relationships from the very beginning.

Expectation.

People rarely meet someone without imagining what that connection might eventually become.

They picture companionship.

Support.

A shared future.

Someone who makes life feel slightly less uncertain.

These hopes are natural.

But they also introduce something complicated.

Because once expectations begin forming, they quietly influence how people see each other.

At first this influence is almost invisible.

Two people are simply enjoying each other's presence.

Conversations feel easy.

Laughter arrives without effort.

Moments of connection appear that feel rare and meaningful.

During this stage imagination tends to move faster than understanding.

People begin filling the unknown spaces with possibilities.

What life might feel like together.

How the future might unfold.

How two separate lives might gradually become one shared experience.

None of this is dishonest.

It is simply human.

The mind has always been good at telling stories about the future.

Especially when hope is involved.

But people are always more complex than the stories we initially create about them.

Everyone carries experiences that are not immediately visible.
But eventually, they begin to surface.

Not all at once.
Not in ways that are easy to recognize.

They appear through reactions.
Through moments that feel slightly more intense than expected.

Through situations that seem simple on the surface, but carry
something deeper underneath.

And this is where relationships begin to change.

Not because something is wrong.
But because something real is finally being revealed.

They reveal themselves slowly.

Usually through situations that seem ordinary at first.

A disagreement.

A misunderstanding.

And something unexpected begins to appear.

Not the situation itself…
but the person beneath it.

Reactions that were never visible before.
Parts of someone that only surface when something feels
uncertain.

And this is when relationships begin moving beyond imagination.

Two individuals are no longer interacting with the versions they
first imagined.

They are beginning to encounter the real person standing in front
of them.

For some relationships this discovery deepens the connection.

Understanding grows.

Patience grows.

Two people slowly learn how to navigate each other's differences.

For others the discovery can feel more confusing.

Because sometimes the person someone believed they understood turns out to be more complicated than expected.

Not worse.

Not better.

Simply more human.

And human beings have always been wonderfully complicated creatures.

Each person arrives carrying a lifetime of experiences that shaped how they see the world.

Experiences that quietly influence how they interpret words.

How they react to disappointment.

How easily they trust.

How quickly they withdraw.

None of these patterns are obvious when people first meet.

They only become visible once two lives begin interacting closely enough to reveal them.

This is why many disagreements in relationships seem confusing at first.

Two people may be discussing something that appears simple on the surface.

A comment.

A forgotten detail.

A moment that one person barely noticed.

And yet the reaction that follows can feel surprisingly intense.

Not because the situation itself is significant.

But because the situation touched something deeper.

A memory.

An insecurity.

An old experience that had never fully disappeared.

Most conflicts in relationships are not really about the moment that appears to start them.

They are about everything that moment quietly represents.

One person may believe they are arguing about time.

Another believes they are arguing about respect.

A third might say the disagreement was about tone.

But beneath those explanations something else is often present.

Something far more personal.

A quiet question that was never spoken directly.

Do you see me clearly?

Do you understand what I carry?

And do we belong in each other's lives?

These questions rarely appear in conversation the way they exist in thought.

They feel too vulnerable.

Too revealing.

Instead they appear indirectly.

Through frustration.

Through defensiveness.

Through moments when a reaction seems larger than the situation itself.

And when two people are both protecting something emotional at the same time, misunderstanding becomes easy.

Each person begins explaining their perspective.

Defending their intentions.

Trying to clarify what they meant.

All the while believing the other person simply does not understand.

Yet very often both people are trying to express the same underlying desire.

To feel heard.

To feel valued.

To feel safe in the connection they are building together.

This is one of the quiet paradoxes of relationships.

Two people may care deeply about each other while simultaneously struggling to recognize what the other person is actually asking for.

Not because either of them lacks empathy.

But because emotional needs are rarely communicated with perfect clarity.

Understanding another person requires patience.

Not the kind of patience that simply waits for disagreement to disappear.

The kind that remains curious.

Curious enough to ask what a reaction might mean beneath the words that were spoken.

Curious enough to notice when someone is trying to express something they may not yet fully understand themselves.

Because relationships are rarely conversations between two perfectly understood individuals.

They are conversations between two evolving lives.

And evolving lives are rarely simple.

But they can be deeply meaningful.

Especially when two people are willing to keep learning about each other long after the first impressions have faded.

Because the earliest version of a relationship is often shaped by discovery.

Everything feels new.

Questions lead to stories.

Stories reveal small pieces of a life that previously existed outside the other person's awareness.

Where someone grew up.

What shaped their interests.

What they hope the future might look like.

During this stage curiosity comes easily.

People want to understand each other.

They listen carefully.

They notice details.

They remember things that might seem insignificant to anyone else.

But familiarity gradually changes the rhythm of that curiosity.

Once two people begin feeling comfortable with each other, they often assume they already understand the person beside them.

The questions become less frequent.

The listening becomes less deliberate.

Not because the connection has weakened.

But because the unknown spaces that once invited curiosity now appear to be filled.

And this is where something subtle begins to happen.

People stop discovering each other.

And start interpreting each other instead.

Interpretation can be useful.

It allows people to anticipate behavior.

To recognize patterns.

To navigate everyday life without needing to explain every small detail.

But interpretation also carries a quiet risk.

Because once someone believes they understand another person, they may begin reacting not to what the person is actually doing…

but to what they expect that behavior to mean.

A simple comment can suddenly feel loaded with intention.

A small oversight can feel like evidence of something larger.

A moment of silence can begin to look like distance.

And yet the other person may have experienced that same moment very differently.

A comment spoken casually.

An oversight caused by distraction.

Silence that simply meant they were thinking.

Two people observing the same moment.

And yet experiencing two completely different meanings.

This is why communication in relationships can feel surprisingly complicated.

Words are shared.

But interpretation is personal.

Every sentence passes through the lens of the listener's experiences before it becomes understanding.

Past relationships.

Past disappointments.

Past moments when trust was broken or misunderstood.

All of these things quietly shape how people hear what is being said.

Even when the person speaking had something entirely different in mind.

For a long time many people assume that misunderstanding means something is wrong.

That two people who care about each other should naturally understand each other without difficulty.

But understanding rarely appears that easily.

It grows slowly.

Through repeated conversations.

Through patience.

Through the willingness to occasionally admit that our first interpretation might not always be the most accurate one.

And when people begin approaching relationships with that kind of humility, something interesting starts to happen.

Disagreements begin to feel less like battles.

And more like invitations to understand something that was previously hidden.

Not every disagreement will reveal something profound.

Sometimes people simply miscommunicate.

Sometimes they are tired.

Sometimes they are distracted.

Human beings are not always perfectly consistent creatures.

But every once in a while a disagreement reveals something deeper.

A fear that had never been spoken.

An expectation that had quietly existed in the background.

A need that the other person did not realize was there.

And in those moments relationships become something far more interesting than simple companionship.

They become a place where two people slowly learn how to understand not only each other…

but themselves.

Because understanding another person often reveals something unexpected about the person doing the understanding.

Reactions that once felt automatic begin to invite curiosity.

Why did that moment feel important?

Why did that comment linger longer than it should have?

Why did something small suddenly feel significant?

These questions rarely have simple answers.

Human emotions are rarely organized into neat explanations.

They are shaped by memories.

Experiences.

Small moments that left impressions long before anyone realized how meaningful they would eventually become.

This is why relationships can sometimes feel like quiet explorations of the past.

Not intentionally.

But inevitably.

Because when two people become close enough, parts of their earlier lives begin appearing in the present.

Old lessons about trust.

Old fears about being misunderstood.

Old hopes about what love might finally feel like.

Most people are not consciously aware of how much of their past travels with them into new relationships.

They believe they are responding to the moment in front of them.

But often the moment is touching something older.

Something that existed long before the current relationship began.

This does not mean people are trapped by their past.

But it does mean the past has a voice.

Sometimes quiet.

Sometimes surprisingly loud.

And relationships tend to give that voice opportunities to speak.

Which is why connection requires something deeper than simple attraction.

Attraction may bring people together.

But understanding is what allows them to remain there.

Understanding requires attention.

The kind of attention that notices not only what someone says…

but how they say it.

What changes when they are comfortable.

What changes when they are uncertain.

What they avoid talking about.

And what seems to matter more than they initially admit.

These details rarely appear all at once.

They reveal themselves slowly.

Often over months.

Sometimes over years.

Because people do not fully understand themselves immediately either.

They discover parts of their own personality gradually.

Through experiences.

Through mistakes.

Through moments when life asks questions they did not previously know existed.

This is why relationships can evolve in unexpected ways.

The two people who first met are not always the same two people who remain years later.

Experiences shape them.

Challenges reshape their priorities.

Time introduces perspectives that were impossible to imagine earlier.

Some relationships grow stronger through this process.

Two people learn how to adapt together.

They become familiar with each other's fears.

Each other's habits.

Each other's quiet ways of seeking reassurance when life feels uncertain.

Other relationships struggle under the same pressure.

Not because either person is flawed.

But because growth sometimes leads people in different directions.

And understanding does not always mean staying.

Sometimes it simply means recognizing when two lives are no longer moving in the same direction.

This realization can be difficult.

Human beings naturally want their stories to continue the way they first imagined them.

They want the connection that once felt promising to remain exactly as it was.

But life rarely remains exactly as it begins.

Change is one of its most consistent qualities.

And relationships, like people, are not immune to that change.

They evolve.

They deepen.

Sometimes they fade.

Sometimes they transform into something different from what either person originally expected.

But even when relationships change, they rarely leave people unchanged.

Every meaningful connection teaches something.

About communication.

About patience.

About the strange and complicated ways human beings try to care for each other.

And perhaps most importantly…

about how much of ourselves we discover through the people we meet along the way.

Because every meaningful connection leaves some kind of trace.

Not always immediately visible.

Sometimes it appears years later.

A way of thinking that changed.

A lesson about patience.

A new understanding of what kindness actually looks like when life becomes complicated.

People often imagine that relationships are defined by how long they last.

But time is only one measure of significance.

Some connections exist for decades and remain surprisingly shallow.

Others appear briefly and leave an impression that quietly shapes the rest of a person's life.

This is one of the reasons human relationships can feel so difficult to understand.

Their importance is rarely obvious while they are unfolding.

People only recognize their influence later.

Looking back at the moments that seemed ordinary at the time.

Conversations that lingered longer than expected.

Small gestures that carried more meaning than anyone realized.

Life has a habit of revealing the significance of relationships in reverse.

Only after distance appears do people begin to see what those connections actually gave them.

Perspective.

Growth.

Sometimes even the courage to become someone slightly different than they were before.

And once someone begins noticing this pattern, relationships start to look less like fixed roles…

and more like chapters in a much larger story.

Some chapters are brief.

Some are long.

Some are joyful.

Others more complicated.

But each one contributes something to the person who continues the journey afterward.

This is why the true value of many relationships is not always visible while they are happening.

People often focus on what they hoped the relationship would become.

Whether it lasted.

Whether it matched the future they once imagined.

But meaning does not always appear in the form people originally expected.

Sometimes the purpose of a connection is simply to change something inside a person.

To challenge an assumption.

To reveal a part of themselves they had never examined before.

To show them what they value more deeply than they realized.

In that way relationships often behave less like permanent structures...

and more like teachers.

Some teach gently.

Through support.

Through encouragement.

Through the quiet reassurance that someone else understands the world in a similar way.

Others teach through difficulty.

Through misunderstanding.

Through the uncomfortable discovery that two people may want very different things from life.

Neither type of lesson is meaningless.

Both leave their mark.

Because every meaningful relationship introduces someone to a new perspective.

Another way of experiencing the world.

Another way of interpreting what matters and what does not.

And when people are open enough to notice those lessons, something interesting begins to happen.

Relationships stop feeling like things that must succeed or fail.

They begin to feel like experiences that shape understanding.

Some people remain in our lives for decades.

Others only for a short chapter.

But every connection that truly mattered leaves something behind.

A memory.

A lesson.

A quiet shift in how we understand ourselves.

And perhaps that is why human beings continue seeking connection despite how complicated it can sometimes be.

Not because relationships are always easy.

But because they reveal parts of life that cannot be discovered alone.

Which means that even when relationships change…

even when they end…

even when two people eventually continue their lives in different directions…

the experience itself rarely disappears.

It simply becomes part of the person who continues forward.

And in that quiet way, every relationship becomes something more than the story people once imagined it would be.

It becomes part of the person they are still becoming.

And perhaps that is one of the quieter truths about human connection.

People rarely leave relationships exactly the way they entered them.

Something always shifts.

Sometimes it is obvious.

A change in how someone approaches love.

A clearer understanding of what they value in another person.

Or a deeper awareness of what they can offer themselves.

Other changes are far more subtle.

A slightly different way of listening.

A greater patience with the imperfections of others.

A recognition that every person carries struggles that may never be fully explained.

These kinds of changes rarely appear dramatic from the outside.

But they quietly reshape the way someone moves through the rest of their life.

How they approach the next relationship.

How they respond when connection feels uncertain.

How they understand the delicate balance between independence and closeness.

Because every relationship leaves behind a small collection of insights.

What kindness looks like when it is genuine.

What respect feels like when it is mutual.

What communication requires when two people truly want to understand each other.

And sometimes, just as importantly, what happens when those things are missing.

These discoveries are not always comfortable.

But they are valuable.

They allow people to approach future connections with a little more awareness than they had before.

Which is perhaps why human beings continue searching for connection even after experiencing disappointment.

Because somewhere inside most people is the quiet
understanding that relationships are not only about
companionship.

They are about growth.

Growth rarely happens in isolation.

It happens through interaction.

Through the friction of different perspectives.

Through the process of learning how another person sees the
world.

And occasionally through the difficult realization that not every
connection can continue forever.

Some relationships change.

Some fade.

Some simply reach the point where two lives are no longer moving
in the same direction.

But even those endings rarely erase the value of what existed
before them.

They simply mark the end of one chapter.

And the beginning of another.

Because life rarely stops introducing new people.

New connections.

New opportunities to understand something about ourselves that we had not yet noticed.

And in that sense, relationships are never only about the people we meet.

They are also about the person we slowly become while meeting them.

Because every meaningful connection leaves behind something that quietly travels with us afterward.

A way of thinking.

A way of listening.

A deeper understanding of what it means to share life with another person.

For a long time many people assume that relationships are meant to provide certainty.

A stable place where confusion disappears.

Where two people finally understand each other completely.

But complete understanding is a rare thing.

Even the closest relationships continue revealing new layers over time.

Because people themselves continue changing.

Experiences reshape them.

Responsibilities reshape them.

Time introduces perspectives that were impossible to imagine earlier in life.

This is why the person someone meets at the beginning of a relationship is rarely the exact same person who remains years later.

Growth quietly alters priorities.

New experiences introduce new questions.

And sometimes the connection must adapt alongside those changes.

The strongest relationships often share one unusual quality.

They allow both people to evolve.

Not by forcing them to remain the same…

but by making space for the changes that naturally arrive with time.

That kind of connection requires something deeper than attraction.

It requires patience.

Trust.

And the willingness to occasionally admit that no one ever fully finishes learning who another person is.

Because understanding someone completely would require understanding every moment that shaped them.

Every memory.

Every disappointment.

Every quiet hope they may never have spoken out loud.

And no relationship, no matter how close, can fully access all of that.

But what it can do is something equally meaningful.

It can create a place where two people gradually become more comfortable revealing those hidden parts of themselves.

This process takes time.

And sometimes it takes courage.

Because revealing the deeper parts of ourselves always carries a certain risk.

The risk that the other person may not understand.

The risk that they may see something they did not expect.

But without that vulnerability, connection rarely deepens beyond the surface.

And surface connections, while pleasant, rarely leave a lasting impression on a person's life.

The relationships that truly shape people are usually the ones where honesty eventually becomes more important than comfort.

Where two individuals become willing to show the parts of themselves that are still uncertain.

Still imperfect.

Still evolving.

Because those are the moments where connection becomes real.

Not a story people imagine about each other.

But an understanding that continues growing as long as both people remain curious about the lives unfolding beside their own.

Curiosity, in many ways, is one of the quiet foundations of lasting connection.

When curiosity remains alive, people continue asking questions.

They continue noticing small changes.

They remain interested in who the other person is becoming, not only who they once appeared to be.

Without curiosity, relationships can slowly begin to feel predictable.

Conversations repeat themselves.

Assumptions replace discovery.

People begin believing they already know everything important about the person beside them.

But no human life is ever completely predictable.

Everyone continues evolving, whether they realize it or not.

New experiences reshape priorities.

Unexpected challenges introduce perspectives that did not exist before.

Moments of reflection quietly alter the way someone understands themselves.

And when curiosity remains present, these changes do not feel threatening.

They feel interesting.

They become opportunities to rediscover someone in a slightly different way.

This is why the healthiest relationships rarely depend on the illusion that two people will remain exactly the same.

Instead they allow space for change.

They allow room for growth.

They accept that life will occasionally introduce situations neither person fully anticipated.

In that sense, relationships are not static agreements.

They are living experiences.

They move.

They adjust.

They respond to the circumstances life introduces along the way.

Sometimes those adjustments bring two people closer.

Shared experiences deepen understanding.

Challenges reveal strengths neither person knew the other possessed.

Moments of vulnerability create a quiet trust that cannot easily be replaced.

Other times life leads people in different directions.

New priorities appear.

New responsibilities emerge.

Paths that once ran side by side slowly begin to separate.

When this happens, it can feel disappointing.

Human beings naturally hope that meaningful connections will last forever.

They imagine that once two people understand each other deeply enough, separation will never become necessary.

But life rarely follows promises that simple.

People change.

Circumstances change.

And sometimes the most honest outcome of a relationship is not permanence…

but gratitude for the time that existed.

This kind of understanding does not always arrive immediately.

It often appears later.

When distance has introduced perspective.

When the intensity of the moment has softened enough to allow reflection.

And with that reflection comes a quieter realization.

Relationships are not only valuable because they continue.

They are valuable because they shape who we become while they exist.

And often the influence of a relationship becomes clearer only after time has passed.

In the moment, people are usually focused on the experience itself.

The conversations.

The emotions.

The effort required to understand another person while being understood in return.

But later, when life has moved forward and distance has appeared, something interesting begins to happen.

People start recognizing what those connections quietly gave them.

A different way of seeing the world.

A deeper patience with the complexity of human emotions.

A clearer understanding of what kind of connection truly matters to them.

Sometimes those realizations arrive gently.

Through quiet reflection.

Through noticing how certain experiences changed the way someone approaches the people they meet afterward.

Other times the realization arrives more suddenly.

A moment when someone recognizes that a past relationship shaped far more of their life than they originally understood.

Not only through the time they spent together.

But through the person they became afterward.

Because relationships do not only exist in the present moment.

They continue influencing the future in subtle ways.

The lessons they leave behind travel forward with the person who experienced them.

Into new friendships.

Into new partnerships.

Into the quiet decisions someone makes about how they want to live.

This is one of the reasons human connection remains such a powerful force in life.

Even brief encounters can leave lasting impressions.

A conversation that changed someone's perspective.

An act of kindness that arrived at the right moment.

A relationship that revealed strengths or vulnerabilities that had never been noticed before.

None of these moments disappear completely.

They become part of a person's understanding of the world.

Part of the story they carry with them as life continues unfolding.

And when people begin recognizing this, something interesting happens to the way they look at relationships.

They stop measuring connection only by how long it lasts.

They begin noticing how deeply it mattered while it existed.

Because sometimes the most meaningful connections are not the ones that remain unchanged forever.

Sometimes they are the ones that appear at exactly the moment they were needed.

Stay long enough to change something important.

And then quietly become part of the life that continues afterward.

In that way, relationships rarely have simple definitions.

They are not always permanent.

They are not always easy.

But they are almost always meaningful.

Because through them, human beings learn something they could never fully discover alone.

They learn how their presence affects another life.

How their words can comfort or wound.

How their patience can strengthen a moment that might otherwise have broken.

These lessons are rarely taught deliberately.

They emerge naturally through interaction.

Through the countless small moments that make up shared experience.

Over time these moments begin forming a quiet understanding.

A recognition that relationships are not simply about finding someone who perfectly fits the life we imagined.

They are about learning how to exist beside another human being whose life is unfolding just as unpredictably as our own.

Two people.

Each carrying their own questions.

Each carrying their own hopes about what connection might bring.

And somehow trying to build something meaningful in the space where those two lives meet.

Sometimes that effort produces something lasting.

A connection that grows deeper as years pass.

A partnership that adapts to the changes life introduces.

Two individuals who continue choosing each other even as the circumstances around them evolve.

Other times the effort reveals something different.

Two people who care about each other, but discover that their paths are gradually leading in different directions.

Not because either person failed.

Not because the connection lacked sincerity.

Simply because life does not always guide two journeys along the same road forever.

Understanding this can take time.

Many people grow up believing that relationships must either succeed completely or fail entirely.

That lasting connection is the only measure of meaning.

But life rarely follows such clear definitions.

Some relationships are meant to last for decades.

Others exist only long enough to reveal something important about the people within them.

And when people begin to see relationships this way, something shifts in how they understand connection.

Instead of asking only how long something will last…

they begin asking what it is teaching them while it exists.

What patience feels like when two people try to understand each other.

What honesty requires when vulnerability becomes unavoidable.

What care looks like when someone chooses to remain present even during moments of difficulty.

These discoveries slowly reshape a person's understanding of love.

Not as something perfect.

Not as something effortless.

But as something human.

Something that grows through attention.

Through curiosity.

Through the willingness to remain open even when understanding takes time.

And perhaps that is why relationships continue to matter so deeply in human life.

Because in the presence of another person, life stops being an abstract idea.

It becomes immediate.

Personal.

Real in ways that no amount of reflection alone could ever fully create.

Because when another person enters our lives, the questions of life stop being theoretical.

They become lived experiences.

Patience is no longer an idea.

It becomes something practiced in small moments.

Understanding is no longer a concept.

It becomes the effort to listen when another person is trying to explain something that matters deeply to them.

Care is no longer a word.

It becomes the quiet decision to remain present even when situations feel complicated.

This is one of the ways relationships change a person.

They transform abstract values into lived behavior.

It is easy to believe we are compassionate until someone tests that compassion.

Easy to believe we are patient until patience becomes necessary.

Easy to believe we understand love until another person asks us to show it in ways we did not expect.

And through these experiences people slowly begin discovering something important.

Relationships are not simply places where life happens.

They are places where character reveals itself.

Sometimes the revelation is encouraging.

People discover strengths they did not know they possessed.

A capacity for kindness that appears naturally when someone else needs it.

A resilience that becomes visible when a relationship passes through difficulty but continues forward.

Other times the revelation is more challenging.

People notice reactions they did not expect.

Impatience.

Defensiveness.

Moments when their own fears shape how they respond to someone they care about.

These discoveries are not always comfortable.

But they are valuable.

Because awareness is often the first step toward growth.

When people begin recognizing their own patterns within relationships, something subtle changes.

They become less focused on judging the other person.

And more curious about understanding themselves.

Why did that moment affect me so strongly?

Why did that misunderstanding feel so important?

What part of my own experience shaped the way I reacted?

These questions transform relationships into something deeper than simple companionship.

They turn connection into a place of reflection.

A place where two people, sometimes without realizing it, help each other grow.

And growth rarely follows a straight path.

There will be moments of harmony.

Moments where understanding flows easily and life feels shared in a natural way.

But there will also be moments of tension.

Moments where differences appear that neither person fully anticipated.

Those moments are not signs that something has failed.

Often they are simply signs that two lives are still learning how to exist beside one another.

Because relationships, like life itself, are not problems waiting to be solved.

They are experiences waiting to be understood.

Because understanding does not always mean permanence.

Some relationships remain part of a person's life for decades.

Others exist only briefly.

Yet both can leave an equally lasting influence.

Human beings often measure relationships by their duration.

How long they lasted.

Whether they continued or eventually ended.

But time alone rarely explains the true significance of a connection.

Some people remain present in our lives for many years and yet leave little lasting impression.

Others appear for a short moment and quietly change the direction of a person's thinking forever.

It is not the length of a relationship that determines its meaning.

It is the depth of the experience it created.

The understanding it introduced.

The part of ourselves it revealed.

And this is why people continue seeking connection even after experiencing disappointment.

Because somewhere inside most individuals exists the quiet knowledge that relationships offer something life cannot provide in any other way.

A mirror.

A challenge.

A shared moment where two lives briefly learn something about themselves through each other.

Some connections remain.

They grow deeper with time.

They adapt as life changes.

They become familiar companions through the unpredictable landscape of years.

Others eventually reach their natural conclusion.

Not always dramatically.

Sometimes simply through the gradual realization that two lives are moving in different directions.

Yet even those endings rarely erase what once existed.

They simply transform the relationship into something different.

A memory.

A lesson.

A quiet influence that continues shaping the person who experienced it.

And perhaps that is the simplest way to understand relationships.

Not as permanent destinations.

But as encounters that help reveal who we are becoming.

And perhaps this is why people continue opening their lives to others despite the uncertainty that relationships inevitably carry.

Because somewhere within every meaningful connection there exists the possibility of discovery.

Not only the discovery of another person…

but the discovery of ourselves.

Who we are when we care deeply about someone.

Who we are when patience is required.

Who we are when disappointment appears and understanding must decide whether to remain.

Relationships quietly ask these questions without ever announcing them directly.

They appear through ordinary moments.

Through conversations that unexpectedly become important.

Through small decisions about how we respond when another person reveals something fragile about their life.

And over time those moments begin shaping something deeper than the relationship itself.

They shape character.

They shape the way someone understands trust.

They shape the quiet expectations a person carries into the next connection they encounter.

Because every meaningful relationship leaves behind more than memories.

It leaves perspective.

A clearer understanding of what matters.

A clearer understanding of what kind of presence we hope to be in the lives of others.

Some of these lessons arrive through joy.

Others arrive through difficulty.

But both carry the same quiet purpose.

They reveal something about what it means to share life with another human being.

And once someone begins to recognize this, relationships start to look different.

Less like fragile arrangements that must remain unchanged forever.

And more like experiences that shape the person continuing forward through life.

Because the truth is that relationships rarely exist only for themselves.

They exist to teach something about the people living inside them.

Attachment changes the way people experience life.

Before it, everything exists at a distance.

People move through their days making decisions that affect only themselves.

Their thoughts remain private.

Their emotions contained within their own perspective.

But once attachment forms, something shifts.

Another person begins to matter.

Not occasionally.

But consistently.

Their presence becomes significant.

Their absence becomes noticeable.

And their well-being begins to carry a weight that did not exist
before.

This is often where love begins to feel real.

Not in the initial excitement.

Not in the early curiosity.

But in the quiet realization that someone else now occupies a
meaningful space within your life.

And with that realization comes something unexpected.

Vulnerability.

Because caring about someone always introduces the possibility
of losing them.

Not necessarily through absence.

But through misunderstanding.

Through distance.

Through the subtle ways two people can drift apart without intending to.

For a long time many people believe love will make life feel more certain.

More stable.

More understood.

But love rarely removes uncertainty.

If anything, it introduces new forms of it.

Now the questions become different.

Not about life in general.

But about connection.

Will this last?

Will this remain as it feels now?

Will this person continue choosing me the same way I am choosing them?

These questions are rarely spoken out loud.

But they exist quietly beneath the surface of many relationships.

Shaping behavior.

Influencing decisions.

Creating moments of hesitation that are difficult to explain.

This is one of the reasons love can feel both comforting and unsettling at the same time.

It brings closeness.

But it also introduces the awareness that something meaningful now exists outside of our direct control.

Because no matter how strong a connection feels, it is still shared between two individuals.

Each with their own thoughts.

Their own emotions.

Their own evolving understanding of what they want from life.

And this is where love begins to require something deeper than feeling.

It requires trust.

Not the kind of trust that guarantees certainty.

But the kind that allows someone to remain present even when certainty is not available.

Because love, like life itself, does not always offer clear answers.

It does not explain itself fully.

It does not guarantee permanence.

And it does not always unfold the way people initially imagine.

Yet people continue choosing it.

Not because it removes uncertainty.

But because it makes life feel more meaningful despite it.

Yet the deeper attachment becomes, the more quietly something else begins to grow alongside it.

Dependence.

Not always obvious.

Not always acknowledged.

But present in subtle ways.

People begin adjusting their emotional state around another person's presence.

A message can shift the mood of an entire day.

A moment of distance can create a quiet sense of unease.

A small change in tone can feel larger than it actually is.

None of this is unusual.

It is simply what happens when someone becomes important.

Because once a person begins to matter, their actions begin to carry meaning beyond the moment itself.

A delay is no longer just a delay.

It becomes a question.

A silence is no longer just silence.

It becomes something to interpret.

And this is where love begins to move beyond connection…

and into attachment.

Attachment is not inherently negative.

It is one of the ways human beings form bonds.

It creates closeness.

It allows people to care deeply about one another.

It gives relationships emotional depth.

But attachment also introduces something else.

Sensitivity.

The more someone cares, the more aware they become of anything that might threaten that connection.

Not always in dramatic ways.

Often in quiet, internal ones.

Small thoughts.

Subtle doubts.

Questions that appear without being invited.

What if this changes?

What if this fades?

What if I lose something that now feels important?

These thoughts are rarely constant.

But they exist.

And when they appear, they reveal something deeper about love.

Love is not only about gaining something meaningful.

It is also about becoming aware that something meaningful can be lost.

And that awareness is what makes love feel both powerful…

and fragile.

Because just like life itself, love does not come with guarantees.

It does not promise permanence.

It does not promise that two people will always remain the same.

And yet people still choose it.

Not because it is certain.

But because of what it offers while it exists.

Moments of understanding.

Moments of closeness.

Moments where life feels shared instead of experienced alone.

This is the quiet exchange at the centre of love.

People accept uncertainty…

in return for meaning.

And as attachment deepens, something else begins to appear more clearly.

The instinct to hold on.

At first, this instinct feels natural.

When something is meaningful, people want to preserve it.

They want to protect it from change.

From distance.

From anything that might slowly alter what once felt certain.

But life rarely remains still long enough for anything to stay exactly the same.

People change.

Circumstances shift.

Priorities evolve in ways that are not always visible at first.

And sometimes, without either person fully intending it, a relationship begins to feel different.

Not necessarily worse.

Not necessarily broken.

Just… different.

These changes are often subtle.

A slight distance where closeness once felt effortless.

Conversations that require a little more effort than before.

Moments where understanding no longer feels automatic.

At first, many people ignore these shifts.

They assume it is temporary.

Something that will pass with time.

Something that does not need to be questioned too closely.

But eventually, the difference becomes difficult to overlook.

And this is where something important begins to happen internally.

One part of a person starts to recognize the change.

Quietly.

Without urgency.

Simply noticing that something is not the same as it once was.

While another part resists that realization.

Holding on to what the connection used to feel like.

Revisiting earlier moments.

Remembering how natural everything once seemed.

This internal tension is one of the most difficult parts of love.

The space between what is…

and what used to be.

Because letting go is rarely about the other person alone.

It is also about letting go of the version of the relationship that once existed.

The version that felt certain.

The version that felt easy.

The version that made sense without effort.

And people do not easily release something that once made their life feel more complete.

So they try to hold it together.

Through effort.

Through patience.

Through the quiet hope that things might return to what they were before.

Sometimes that effort brings two people closer again.

Understanding returns.

Communication deepens.

The connection finds a new balance.

But other times, the effort only reveals something more difficult.

That the relationship has already begun to move in a different direction.

And this is where one of the hardest realizations in love begins to form.

Not everything that was once meaningful is meant to remain unchanged.

Because love, like life, does not always follow the path people hoped it would.

It unfolds in ways that are not always predictable.

Not always controllable.

And not always aligned with the version people imagined at the beginning.

And even when change becomes visible, people do not always leave.

Not immediately.

Sometimes not at all.

Because leaving is rarely just a decision.

It is a process.

One that unfolds slowly.

Often quietly.

And not always in a straight line.

For a long time, people remain in what once was.

Not because they cannot see what is changing…

but because they remember what it used to be.

They remember how natural the connection felt.

How easily conversations flowed.

How certain everything seemed at the beginning.

And those memories carry weight.

They create a sense of continuity.

A belief that what once existed might still be possible again.

So people stay.

Not out of confusion.

But out of hope.

Hope that the distance is temporary.

Hope that the misunderstanding can be resolved.

Hope that the version of the relationship they once experienced has not completely disappeared.

And hope is a powerful force.

It allows people to endure uncertainty longer than they otherwise might.

It allows them to remain present in situations that feel unclear.

It allows them to believe in possibilities that are not yet visible.

But hope can also make it difficult to see things as they are.

Because when someone is holding on to what something used to feel like…

it becomes harder to fully accept what it has become.

This creates a quiet conflict within a person.

Two understandings existing at the same time.

One that sees the present clearly.

Recognizing the distance.

The changes.

The subtle ways the connection no longer feels the same.

And another that remains connected to the past.

Holding on to the memory of what once existed.

This tension is not easy to resolve.

Because neither side is entirely wrong.

The past was real.

The connection was real.

The meaning it carried did not disappear simply because
something changed.

But the present is also real.

And it asks for something different.

To see clearly.

To acknowledge what is no longer the same.

To recognize that not everything meaningful is meant to remain unchanged forever.

This is where love becomes one of the most difficult experiences to navigate.

Not when everything feels right.

But when something begins to shift, and clarity arrives slowly.

Because clarity does not always appear all at once.

It comes in moments.

Small realizations.

Subtle recognitions that something has changed, even if it cannot yet be fully explained.

And in those moments, people begin to understand something that is both simple and difficult at the same time.

Staying is not always the same as preserving something.

Sometimes it is simply delaying the moment of acceptance.

Because not everything that can be understood can be held onto.

And not everything that once made sense will continue to.

And sometimes the most difficult part is not understanding what is happening.

It is accepting what is already understood.

Because there are moments in relationships where the answer becomes quietly clear.

Not through a single event.

Not through something obvious.

But through a gradual accumulation of small realizations.

A pattern that no longer feels the same.

A distance that does not fully close.

A sense that something meaningful has shifted, even if it has not been openly acknowledged.

These moments do not arrive with certainty.

They arrive with hesitation.

With quiet awareness.

With a feeling that is difficult to explain, but difficult to ignore.

And in those moments, many people already know.

They understand that something has changed.

That the connection is no longer what it once was.

That the direction of the relationship may no longer be the same.

But knowing is not the same as accepting.

Because acceptance asks for something more difficult.

It asks for the willingness to let go of what was once meaningful.

To release the version of the relationship that still exists in memory.

To step away from something that once felt important.

And that is not something people do easily.

So instead, they remain in between.

Between clarity and hope.

Between understanding and resistance.

Between what they know…

and what they are ready to admit.

This space can last for a long time.

Longer than people expect.

Because it is not governed by logic.

It is governed by emotion.

Emotion moves differently.

More slowly.

More carefully.

Sometimes circling the same realization again and again before finally allowing it to settle.

During this time, people may continue the relationship as if nothing has changed.

They may speak the same words.

Follow the same routines.

Hold on to the same patterns.

But internally, something feels different.

A quiet awareness that does not disappear.

A recognition that something meaningful is no longer fully aligned with what it once was.

And this is one of the most human experiences within love.

Not the beginning.

Not the ending.

But the moment in between.

Where clarity exists…

but acceptance has not yet arrived.

Because not every realization asks to be acted on immediately.

Some simply ask to be understood first.

And eventually, something begins to shift.

Not suddenly.

Not dramatically.

But quietly.

Acceptance does not arrive as a decision.

It arrives as a feeling.

A gradual softening of resistance.

A subtle change in how a person relates to what they already know.

The same thoughts are still there.

The same understanding.

The same quiet awareness that something has changed.

But the tension surrounding those thoughts begins to loosen.

What once felt impossible to accept…

starts to feel unavoidable.

And with that shift comes something unexpected.

A sense of loss.

Even before anything has fully ended.

Because people are not only attached to what is happening in the present.

They are attached to what the relationship represented.

What it promised.

What it once felt like.

So when acceptance begins, it does not only acknowledge what is.

It also begins to release what could have been.

And that is where the feeling of loss often begins.

Not at the moment of separation.

But at the moment of realization.

The realization that something meaningful is no longer the same.

The realization that the future once imagined may not unfold in the way it was hoped.

The realization that a version of life is quietly disappearing.

This kind of loss is difficult to explain.

Because nothing has necessarily ended yet.

There may still be communication.

Still be presence.

Still be connection in some form.

But internally, something has shifted.

The certainty that once existed is no longer there.

And in its place is a quiet understanding.

That things are changing.

And with that understanding comes a different kind of emotion.

Not dramatic.

Not overwhelming.

But steady.

A quiet sadness.

Not only for what is happening.

But for what once existed.

For the version of the relationship that felt effortless.

For the moments that now exist only in memory.

For the sense of clarity that once made everything feel simple.

And this sadness does not mean something has failed.

It simply means something mattered.

Because the more something matters,
the more its change can be felt.

And slowly, without a clear moment to point to, something begins
to release.

Not all at once.

Not in a way that feels decisive.

But gradually.

The need to hold on softens.

The urgency to restore what once existed becomes quieter.

The questions that once demanded answers begin to lose their
intensity.

It is not that the meaning disappears.

It is that the resistance begins to fade.

People often imagine letting go as something dramatic.

A final decision.

A clear ending.

A moment where everything changes at once.

But more often, letting go happens internally.

In small, almost unnoticed ways.

A thought that no longer lingers as long.

A memory that feels softer than it once did.

A realization that settles instead of resisting.

And over time, these small shifts begin to change the way someone carries the relationship within them.

What once felt immediate…

begins to feel distant.

Not unimportant.

Not forgotten.

Just no longer present in the same way.

This is the quiet nature of letting go.

It does not erase what existed.

It changes how it is held.

This is the quiet nature of letting go.

It does not erase what existed.

It changes how it is held.

And with that shift comes something unexpected.

Space.

Space for new thoughts.

New experiences.

New ways of understanding what connection can look like moving forward.

This space is not always comfortable at first.

It can feel unfamiliar.

Even empty.

Because something that once occupied emotional attention is no longer there in the same way.

But over time, that space begins to feel different.

Less like absence.

And more like possibility.

Not a replacement for what was lost.

But an opening for what may eventually come.

Because meaning does not disappear when something ends.

It changes form.

And perhaps that is what letting go truly is.

Not forgetting.

Not removing the past.

But allowing it to exist without needing it to remain the same.

Loss rarely arrives the way people expect it to.

Not always suddenly.

Not always dramatically.

Sometimes it begins quietly.

Long before anything has fully disappeared.

A subtle shift.

A distance that cannot quite be explained.

A sense that something meaningful is no longer as present as it once was.

In these moments, loss does not feel like an event.

It feels like a realization.

Something that slowly becomes clear rather than something that happens all at once.

And because of this, many people do not recognize it immediately.

They continue moving forward as if everything remains unchanged.

They follow the same routines.

Engage in the same conversations.

Hold on to the same expectations.

But internally, something feels different.

A quiet awareness that something once certain is no longer the same.

This is often how loss first appears.

Not as absence.

But as change.

Because before something is gone completely…

it usually begins by becoming less present.

Less certain.

Less familiar.

Less like what it once was.

And this gradual shift can be difficult to understand.

Because nothing has fully ended.

And yet something is no longer entirely there.

This is one of the more complex aspects of loss.

It does not always begin with a clear moment.

It often begins with a feeling.

A feeling that something is moving away.

Even if it has not yet disappeared.

At first, many people try to ignore this feeling.

They assume it will pass.

That things will return to how they were.

That the sense of distance is temporary.

But over time, the feeling becomes harder to dismiss.

And with that comes a quiet realization.

Something meaningful is changing.

And when absence finally becomes real, it rarely announces itself.

It does not arrive with a clear introduction.

It simply appears.

In small moments.

A conversation that no longer happens.

A message that is no longer expected.

A presence that used to be there… now quietly missing.

At first, these moments feel unfamiliar.

Almost temporary.

As if something has simply been delayed.

People continue reaching for what used to exist.

Not consciously.

But through habit.

Through routine.

Through the quiet patterns that once included someone else.

And then, slowly, the realization settles.

This is not a pause.

This is absence.

And absence has a different kind of weight.

Not always heavy.

But persistent.

It appears in ordinary places.

In moments that were once shared.

In thoughts that still include someone who is no longer there in the same way.

This is what makes loss difficult to define.

Because it is not only about what is gone.

It is about everything that remains…

without what used to be part of it.

A day continues.

But it feels slightly different.

A space remains.

But it feels quieter than before.

Nothing stops.

And yet something is missing.

This contrast is what gives loss its particular feeling.

Life continues forward.

But not in the same way.

And over time, people begin to notice something else.

Loss is not only about absence.

It is about memory.

Because what once existed does not simply disappear.

It remains present in a different form.

In thoughts.

In reflections.

In small moments where something reminds a person of what used to be.

These reminders are not always intentional.

They appear unexpectedly.

A place.

A sound.

A detail that connects the present moment to something that once felt familiar.

And in those moments, the past feels close again.

Not fully returned.

But not entirely gone either.

This is the quiet complexity of loss.

Something can be absent…

and still feel present at the same time.

Because memory does not behave in a single way.

It does not simply comfort.

And it does not only cause pain.

It does both.

Often at the same time.

There are moments when memory feels gentle.

A reminder of something meaningful.

A quiet appreciation for what once existed.

In those moments, the past does not feel distant.

It feels present in a softer way.

As if something important has not been lost entirely.

Only changed.

But there are other moments when memory feels heavier.

Less like a reflection…

and more like a contrast.

A comparison between what once was…

and what is now.

And in that comparison, something becomes clear.

The difference.

The absence feels more defined.

More real.

More difficult to ignore.

This is why memory can be both comforting and painful.

It brings something back...

only to remind us that it cannot fully return.

And people often move between these two experiences without realizing it.

One moment feeling grateful for what existed.

Another moment feeling the weight of what is no longer there.

Neither experience is wrong.

Both are part of how human beings process loss.

Because memory is not trying to resolve anything.

It is simply holding onto what mattered.

And what mattered rarely disappears easily.

It stays.

In thoughts.

In quiet reflections.

In the subtle ways a person continues carrying something forward even when it is no longer present in their life.

This is why loss does not feel like a single moment.

It feels like something that continues.

Not constantly.

But repeatedly.

In waves.

Moments where everything feels manageable.

Followed by moments where the absence becomes noticeable again.

And over time, people begin to understand something about these waves.

They are not signs of something being wrong.

They are part of how something meaningful is being remembered.

Because what shapes us does not leave easily.

It remains…

even when the person or moment is no longer there.

And over time, people begin to notice something that is not often spoken about directly.

They do not really move on from loss.

Not in the way they once expected.

There is no clear moment where something that mattered simply disappears from their life completely.

No point where the memory loses all meaning.

No point where the absence becomes irrelevant.

Instead, something else happens.

They learn how to carry it.

At first, this idea can feel discouraging.

People often hope that time will remove the weight entirely.

That eventually everything will return to how it felt before.

But life rarely returns to what it was.

It continues forward.

And within that forward movement, loss does not vanish.

It becomes part of the person moving through life.

Not always at the center of their attention.

Not always something they think about every day.

But present.

In a quieter way.

Like something that has settled rather than disappeared.

This is why the phrase "moving on" can feel incomplete.

Because it suggests leaving something behind entirely.

But what truly mattered is rarely left behind.

It is carried forward.

In different ways.

In the way someone understands connection.

In the way they appreciate moments that might have once felt ordinary.

In the way they recognize the importance of things they once overlooked.

Loss changes perspective.

It introduces a depth that did not exist before.

A different awareness of time.

Of presence.

Of what it means for something to matter while it is still there.

And this awareness does not remove the memory.

It transforms it.

What once felt like immediate presence becomes something else.

Something integrated.

Something that exists as part of a person's understanding rather than something they are trying to hold onto.

This is how loss becomes less overwhelming over time.

Not because it disappears.

But because it finds a place within the person experiencing it.

A place where it can exist without needing constant attention.

Because loss does not remove meaning.

It reshapes it.

And as loss settles into a quieter presence, something else begins to change.

The way people see time.

Moments that once felt ordinary begin to feel different in reflection.

Conversations that seemed small at the time begin to carry more meaning.

Details that once passed unnoticed begin to stand out when remembered.

Because loss has a way of revealing what mattered.

Not through explanation.

But through absence.

What is no longer there becomes more visible in memory.

And in that visibility, people begin to recognize something they may not have fully understood before.

How much of life is experienced without being noticed.

How many moments pass without being fully seen.

Without being fully felt.

Without being fully appreciated for what they are while they are happening.

This realization does not always arrive comfortably.

It can carry a quiet weight.

A recognition that something meaningful existed…

and was not fully understood at the time.

But alongside that weight, something else begins to appear.

Awareness.

A deeper attention to the present.

A subtle shift in how people experience moments as they happen.

Because once someone understands how quickly something meaningful can change…

they begin to notice what is still here.

Not with urgency.

But with clarity.

A conversation feels more present.

Time spent with another person feels more intentional.

Even ordinary moments begin to carry a quiet significance.

This is one of the ways loss changes a person.

It alters how they experience what remains.

Not by making life heavier.

But by making it more visible.

Because when something meaningful has been lost…

what is still present begins to feel different.

More immediate.

More real.

And in that shift, something important begins to develop.

An understanding that life is not only about what continues.

But about what exists now.

Because understanding often arrives too late for what has already passed.

But it can still shape how we experience what remains.

And eventually, something settles.

Not the loss itself.

But the way it is carried.

The intensity softens.

The sharpness of certain moments becomes less immediate.

The feeling that once seemed overwhelming begins to move more quietly through daily life.

This does not mean the loss has disappeared.

It simply means it no longer needs to be resisted in the same way.

Because over time, people begin to understand something that is difficult to explain at first.

Loss does not require resolution.

It requires space.

Space to exist without needing to be constantly examined.

Space to be remembered without needing to be relived.

Space to be part of life without defining it entirely.

And when that space is allowed, something shifts.

The relationship with the loss changes.

It is no longer something that interrupts life.

It becomes something that exists within it.

Quietly.

Steadily.

A part of the person, rather than something separate from them.

And in that way, loss becomes less about what is missing…

and more about what remains.

The impact.

The meaning.

The way it shaped how someone sees the world moving forward.

Because even though something is no longer present in the same way…

its influence continues.

In perspective.

In awareness.

In the quiet ways a person carries what mattered into everything that comes next.

This is what acceptance often looks like.

Not a moment of closure.

But a gradual ability to live alongside what cannot be changed.

To move forward without needing the past to be different.

To remember without being held in place by what is no longer there.

Because what is lost does not disappear.

It becomes part of the life that continues.

And perhaps that is what people slowly learn about loss.

Not how to remove it.

But how to live with it.

Time is one of the few things people experience constantly…

and understand only gradually.

It is always present.

Always moving.

Always shaping life in ways that are not immediately visible.

And yet, for much of life, people do not think about it directly.

In earlier years, time feels expansive.

Open.

Almost limitless.

There is always more of it.

More days ahead.

More opportunities.

More chances to try again if something does not work out the first time.

Decisions feel less permanent.

Mistakes feel less final.

Because there is a quiet assumption that time will continue providing new possibilities.

And in that stage of life, people often move quickly.

From one experience to another.

From one idea to the next.

Without always stopping to consider how time is shaping those moments as they pass.

But as life continues, something begins to change.

Time no longer feels as open as it once did.

Not in a way that is immediately obvious.

But gradually.

People begin noticing how quickly certain periods seem to pass.

Years that once felt long now seem to move faster.

Moments that once felt distant now arrive sooner than expected.

And with that shift comes a different kind of awareness.

That time is not only something we move through.

It is something that moves through us.

It shapes perspective.

It changes priorities.

It alters how people understand what matters.

Things that once felt important may begin to feel less significant.

And things that were once overlooked may begin to carry more meaning.

This change does not happen all at once.

It unfolds slowly.

Through experience.

Through reflection.

Through the quiet accumulation of moments that gradually reshape how life is understood.

And as this awareness begins to develop, people often notice something difficult to explain at first.

Time seems to move faster.

Not in a measurable way.

Not in the sense that days become shorter.

But in how those days are experienced.

Moments that once felt long now pass quickly.

Years that once felt distant now seem to arrive without warning.

And this shift can feel unsettling.

Because it introduces a new understanding of time.

That it is not experienced equally throughout life.

In earlier years, many moments feel new.

New experiences.

New environments.

New emotions that have not yet been fully understood.

And because of that, time feels slower.

More detailed.

More noticeable.

Each experience stands out.

Each moment carries a sense of discovery.

But as life continues, familiarity begins to increase.

Experiences repeat.

Environments become known.

Routines begin to form.

And when moments become familiar, they begin to pass with less attention.

Less attention…

and therefore less awareness of time as it moves.

This is one of the reasons time feels faster.

Not because it is moving differently.

But because it is being noticed less.

And this realization introduces something important.

The experience of time is closely connected to attention.

What is noticed feels longer.

What is overlooked feels brief.

This is why certain moments remain vivid in memory.

They were fully experienced.

Fully present.

And why other periods seem to disappear quickly.

They passed without being fully observed.

Because what is not fully noticed often feels as though it never fully existed.

And as awareness of time deepens, something else begins to change alongside it.

What people value.

Things that once felt urgent begin to feel less important.

And things that were once overlooked begin to stand out more clearly.

In earlier stages of life, attention is often directed outward.

Toward achievement.

Toward progress.

Toward the idea of building something that will define the future.

People measure time through what they accomplish.

What they gain.

What they become.

But as time continues, the way it is measured begins to shift.

It is no longer only about what is achieved.

It becomes about what is experienced.

Moments of connection.

Moments of quiet.

Moments that feel meaningful not because they lead somewhere…

but because of how they are felt while they are happening.

This shift is subtle.

It does not always happen consciously.

But it changes the way people move through life.

They begin to notice things they once overlooked.

A conversation that feels genuine.

Time spent without distraction.

The presence of people who matter in ways that cannot be easily explained.

These moments do not necessarily stand out in a dramatic way.

But they carry a different kind of weight.

Because as awareness of time increases, so does the understanding that not every moment repeats.

And this understanding changes how those moments are experienced.

They become more intentional.

More present.

More noticed.

Not out of urgency.

But out of recognition.

A recognition that time is not only something that continues.

It is something that passes.

And once that becomes clear, life begins to feel slightly different.

Less like something to be rushed through.

And more like something to be observed while it unfolds.

Because what is understood too late can still change how we experience what remains.

And as time continues to move, people begin to notice something else that is not always easy to describe.

They do not feel as old as time suggests.

From the outside, age appears measurable.

Years pass.

Numbers increase.

Life progresses through visible stages.

But internally, the experience is different.

The same thoughts remain.

The same sense of self continues.

The same awareness that has always existed still feels present.

And this creates an interesting contrast.

A person can look at their life and recognize how much time has passed...

while still feeling, in many ways, like the same individual they have always been.

This is one of the quieter aspects of aging.

The external changes are visible.

But the internal experience often feels continuous.

It does not reset.

It does not begin again.

It simply continues, carrying everything that came before it.

And within that continuity, something begins to accumulate.

Experience.

Not just in the form of events.

But in understanding.

In perspective.

In the way someone begins to see patterns that were not visible earlier in life.

Situations that once felt confusing begin to feel familiar.

Reactions that once felt overwhelming begin to feel more manageable.

Not because life becomes simpler.

But because the person experiencing it has changed.

They have seen similar moments before.

Felt similar emotions.

Navigated similar uncertainties.

And through that repetition, something develops.

A quieter way of understanding life.

Less reactive.

Less urgent.

More observant.

Because time does not only move forward.

It deepens perception.

Because over time, everything that is experienced becomes part of how life is seen.

And as time continues to pass, people begin to spend more moments looking back.

Not always intentionally.

Sometimes through memory.

Sometimes through comparison.

Sometimes simply through noticing how different life once felt.

The past does not appear all at once.

It returns in fragments.

A memory of a place.

A version of oneself that feels both familiar and distant.

A moment that once seemed ordinary, now carrying unexpected significance.

And in these reflections, something becomes clear.

Life rarely unfolds the way it was once imagined.

The plans that once felt certain shift.

The expectations change.

The path moves in directions that were not always anticipated.

At first, this can feel surprising.

Even unsettling.

Because earlier in life, people often believe that if they make the right decisions…

life will follow a predictable course.

But time reveals something different.

Life is not built from perfect plans.

It is shaped by moments.

By decisions made with limited understanding.

By circumstances that could not have been predicted in advance.

And when people begin to look back with this awareness, something changes in how they interpret their past.

Instead of judging it…

they begin to understand it.

They see why certain choices were made.

Why certain paths were followed.

Why certain mistakes were necessary for the perspective they now carry.

And this understanding softens something.

The need to rewrite the past.

Because the past no longer feels like something that should have been different.

It becomes something that led to the person who is reflecting on it now.

Because life is often understood most clearly when looking back at it.

And over time, reflection begins to lead somewhere quieter.

Toward acceptance.

Not the kind of acceptance that arrives as a decision.

But the kind that settles gradually.

The past no longer feels like something to question.

The future no longer feels like something that must be controlled.

And the present begins to feel more complete on its own.

This shift is subtle.

But it changes everything.

Because when someone stops trying to hold time in place…

they begin to move with it instead.

Moments are no longer rushed.

They are noticed.

Experiences are no longer measured only by what they lead to.

They are understood for what they are while they exist.

And life begins to feel less like something that is slipping away…

and more like something that is unfolding.

This does not remove the awareness that time is passing.

It deepens it.

But the feeling attached to that awareness changes.

It becomes less about urgency.

And more about presence.

Because once someone understands that time cannot be held…

they begin to value what can be experienced within it.

A conversation.

A moment of quiet.

A connection that exists without needing to last forever to be meaningful.

These things begin to feel complete in themselves.

Because time was never something to hold onto.

Only something to move through.

And perhaps that is what time slowly teaches.

Not how to keep it…

but how to experience it.

Identity is something most people believe they understand early in life…

even though it is still being formed.

At first, it feels simple.

A collection of traits.

Preferences.

Beliefs that seem clear and consistent.

People describe themselves with certainty.

Who they are.

What they value.

What they believe about the world.

And for a time, this sense of identity feels stable.

But much of it is shaped by context.

The environment someone grows up in.

The people they are surrounded by.

The expectations they absorb before they have had the chance to question them.

In those early stages, identity is often inherited before it is examined.

Ideas are accepted because they are familiar.

Behaviors are repeated because they are reinforced.

Beliefs feel true because they have not yet been challenged.

And so a version of the self begins to form.

Not intentionally.

But gradually.

Layer by layer.

And for a while, that version feels complete.

Until life begins to introduce something different.

Contradiction.

Experiences that do not align with what someone once believed.

Situations that challenge the way they understand themselves.

Moments where their reactions surprise them.

And in those moments, identity begins to feel less certain.

Not broken.

But questioned.

Because what once felt fixed…

starts to reveal itself as something more flexible than expected.

Because the person we believe we are is often something we are still learning.

And when identity begins to feel uncertain, something else quietly begins to take shape.

Ego.

Not always in the way people commonly describe it.

Not arrogance.

Not necessarily pride.

But a subtle need to maintain a consistent version of oneself.

A need to feel certain about who we are.

To protect the image we have built over time.

To avoid anything that might challenge that image too directly.

Because once a person begins to question their identity,
something deeper is affected.

Stability.

The sense that the world makes sense in a predictable way.

That actions align with beliefs.

That the person they have been is the person they understand
themselves to be.

Ego exists, in part, to preserve that stability.

It resists contradiction.

It avoids discomfort.

It explains away experiences that do not fit the current
understanding of the self.

Not out of weakness.

But out of instinct.

Because uncertainty about identity can feel disorienting.

So the mind begins to protect itself.

It justifies decisions.

Reframes situations.

Finds reasons why something that challenges the self is not
entirely accurate.

This is why people often defend ideas that no longer fully align with
their experience.

Not because those ideas are still true…

but because they once were.

And letting go of them would mean acknowledging change.

Which is not always easy.

Because change in belief is not only intellectual.

It is personal.

It requires someone to admit that the version of themselves they
once trusted…

was incomplete.

Because the hardest things to let go of are often the beliefs we used to define ourselves.

And over time, another difference begins to reveal itself.

The difference between who people believe they are…

and how they actually behave.

Most individuals carry a clear image of themselves.

They believe they are patient.

Kind.

Understanding.

Rational in the way they approach life.

And in many moments, this image feels accurate.

But there are situations where something else appears.

A reaction that feels sharper than expected.

A response that does not align with what they believed about themselves.

A moment where their behavior seems to contradict the identity they have built.

These moments are often dismissed at first.

Seen as exceptions.

Temporary reactions.

Situations that do not reflect who they "truly" are.

And sometimes, that may be true.

But when similar patterns begin to repeat, something becomes harder to ignore.

That behavior is not always separate from identity.

It is part of it.

Because identity is not only what a person believes about themselves.

It is what they consistently do.

Not in ideal situations.

But in difficult ones.

Not when everything feels calm.

But when something challenges them.

These are the moments where identity becomes visible.

Not as an idea.

But as action.

And this can be uncomfortable to recognize.

Because it means that the image someone holds of themselves…

may not always be complete.

It may highlight certain qualities…

while overlooking others.

Qualities that only appear under pressure.

Under stress.

Under situations that were not anticipated.

Because what we do in difficult moments often reveals more than what we believe about ourselves in calm ones.

And eventually, if someone pays enough attention, something begins to happen.

They start to see themselves more clearly.

Not only the parts they are comfortable with.

But the parts they have not fully acknowledged.

The reactions they once dismissed.

The patterns they once ignored.

The behaviors that did not fit the image they preferred to believe.

At first, this kind of awareness can feel unsettling.

Because it removes something familiar.

The comfort of certainty.

It becomes harder to say, "this is who I am,"
when the evidence begins to show something more complex.

And complexity is not always easy to accept.

It introduces contradiction.

A person can be kind…

and still react with impatience.

They can be understanding…

and still struggle to listen when something challenges them.

They can believe they are honest…

and still avoid truths that feel uncomfortable to face.

None of these contradictions make a person false.

They make them human.

But recognizing that is not always immediate.

Because the ego often steps in at this point.

It begins to explain.

To justify.

To protect the version of the self that feels more comfortable to hold onto.

"This was just a bad moment."

"That situation was different."

"That's not really who I am."

And sometimes those explanations are partly true.

But sometimes they also serve another purpose.

To avoid looking too closely.

Because seeing oneself clearly requires something difficult.

Honesty without defense.

The kind of honesty that does not immediately try to correct or explain what is seen.

But simply allows it to be observed.

And this is where many people hesitate.

Not because they are incapable of awareness.

But because awareness without judgment can feel unfamiliar.

Most people are used to either defending themselves…

or criticizing themselves.

But simply observing…

without immediately reacting…

is something else entirely.

Because understanding ourselves requires the same patience we often try to give others.

And when someone begins to look at themselves without immediately defending what they see, something changes.

The need to protect every part of their identity begins to soften.

Not because they no longer care who they are.

But because they begin to understand that who they are is not fixed in the way they once believed.

It is something that can be observed.

Understood.

Adjusted over time.

This shift creates a different kind of relationship with the self.

Less rigid.

Less defined by a single version of identity.

More open.

Because when a person no longer feels the need to maintain a perfect image of themselves, they gain something unexpected.

Flexibility.

The ability to recognize patterns without immediately resisting them.

The ability to notice reactions without needing to justify them.

The ability to accept that they are still learning who they are.

And within that acceptance, something else begins to appear.

Responsibility.

Not in the sense of blame.

But in the sense of ownership.

An understanding that while past experiences may have shaped certain behaviors…

those behaviors are still part of how they move through the present.

And once something is seen clearly, it becomes difficult to ignore.

Which creates a new possibility.

Change.

Not forced.

Not immediate.

But gradual.

Because awareness naturally influences behavior over time.

When someone begins to notice how they react in certain situations…

they begin to respond differently.

Not perfectly.

But with more intention.

With more understanding of what is actually happening beneath the surface.

Because growth is not only about what happens to us.

It is about how we understand what happens within us.

And over time, this understanding begins to settle into something quieter.

Identity no longer feels like something that needs to be fixed or defended.

It becomes something that is observed.

A reflection of how a person has lived.

How they have reacted.

How they have adapted to the experiences that shaped them.

And because of that, it becomes something that can change.

Not suddenly.

Not dramatically.

But gradually.

As new experiences introduce new perspectives.

As awareness reveals patterns that were once unnoticed.

As understanding replaces the need to remain the same.

This does not remove the sense of self.

It deepens it.

Because a person is no longer defined only by what they believe about themselves.

They are shaped by what they are willing to see.

The more clearly they see…

the more honestly they understand.

And the more honestly they understand…

the more naturally change begins to occur.

Not as an effort to become someone else.

But as a quiet movement toward something more aligned.

More aware.

More consistent with what they have come to understand about themselves.

This is where identity becomes less rigid.

Less about holding onto a fixed idea of who we are…

and more about allowing that idea to evolve.

Because the self is not something that is discovered once.

It is something that is continuously understood.

Because who we are is not something to define once.

Only something to understand as it unfolds.

And perhaps that is what people slowly realize about identity.

Not who they are…

but how they are becoming.

Letting go is often misunderstood.

Not as an action…

but as a loss.

People associate it with giving up.

With something ending.

With the absence of what once mattered.

And because of that, they resist it.

They hold on longer than they need to.

Not because they are unaware…

but because letting go feels like something is being taken from them.

But letting go is not something that happens to a person.

It is something they allow.

A shift in how they relate to what they are holding onto.

Because what most people struggle with is not the thing itself.

It is their attachment to it.

An expectation.

A version of how something was supposed to unfold.

A belief that something meaningful must remain the same in order to continue having value.

And when that expectation is no longer aligned with reality…

the instinct is to hold on tighter.

To preserve what once existed.

To resist what is changing.

To delay the moment where something must be seen clearly.

But holding on does not stop change.

It only makes the experience of it more difficult.

Because change continues regardless.

Quietly.

Steadily.

And the more it is resisted…

the more tension is created.

This tension is often mistaken for loss itself.

But it is something else.

It is the distance between what is…

and what someone wishes it still was.

Because letting go begins the moment that distance is no longer resisted.

And when that resistance begins to soften, something else becomes visible.

Letting go is not about removing something from life.

It is about changing the way it is held.

Because what mattered does not disappear.

The memory remains.

The experience remains.

The meaning remains.

But the need for it to stay the same…

begins to fade.

This is where the shift happens.

Not in what exists.

But in how it is carried.

At first, this can feel unfamiliar.

People are used to holding tightly.

To preserving what they value.

To maintaining a sense of continuity in the things that matter most
to them.

But not everything can be held in that way.

Some things change.

Some things move.

Some things exist only for a certain period of time.

And when that becomes clear, letting go no longer feels like a loss of the thing itself.

It becomes a release of the need for it to remain unchanged.

This does not reduce its importance.

It clarifies it.

Because something does not need to last forever to have been meaningful.

And once that is understood, something else becomes possible.

Peace.

Not the absence of memory.

Not the absence of feeling.

But the absence of tension.

The absence of the constant effort to hold onto something that is already changing.

Because what mattered does not disappear when it changes.

It simply exists differently.

And as letting go becomes clearer, another word often begins to appear alongside it.

Surrender.

A word many people misunderstand.

It is often associated with weakness.

With giving up.

With losing control.

But true surrender is something very different.

It is not the absence of strength.

It is the absence of resistance.

Because there is a difference between choosing not to hold on…

and being unable to.

Surrender is a decision.

A recognition that not everything needs to be controlled in order to be understood.

That not everything needs to remain the same in order to have meaning.

That not every outcome needs to be shaped according to expectation.

At first, this can feel uncomfortable.

People are used to directing their lives.

To making decisions.

To influencing outcomes.

And in many areas, that effort is necessary.

But there are aspects of life that do not respond to control in the same way.

Time.

Change.

The behavior of others.

The way certain situations unfold despite intention.

These things move independently.

And when someone tries to control what cannot be controlled, something else begins to happen.

Tension.

A constant effort to adjust something that is not responding.

A continuous attempt to hold something in place that is already shifting.

This effort can feel like strength.

But often, it is simply resistance.

And resistance, over time, becomes exhausting.

Surrender is what happens when that exhaustion is no longer necessary.

Not because someone has given up.

But because they have understood something important.

That control is not always the same as clarity.

Because not everything needs to be controlled to be meaningful.

And when the need to control begins to loosen, something else gradually takes its place.

Trust.

Not the kind of trust that assumes everything will work out perfectly.

Not the kind that guarantees specific outcomes.

But a quieter form of trust.

The kind that allows life to unfold without needing to shape every moment in advance.

At first, this can feel unfamiliar.

Because much of what people have learned about navigating life is based on control.

Planning.

Predicting.

Trying to ensure that things move in a particular direction.

And in many situations, that effort is useful.

But there are moments where control reaches its limit.

Where no amount of planning changes the outcome.

Where no amount of effort prevents change from happening.

And in those moments, something shifts.

The realization that life continues…

even without control.

That moments still arrive.

Experiences still unfold.

Meaning still appears in unexpected ways.

And when someone begins to trust that process, something changes in how they move through life.

They become less focused on forcing outcomes.

And more open to experiencing what is already happening.

This does not mean passivity.

It does not mean doing nothing.

It means acting where action is possible…

and allowing where it is not.

This balance is subtle.

But it changes the experience of life completely.

Because when someone is no longer constantly trying to control everything…

they begin to notice more.

Moments feel less rushed.

Experiences feel less pressured.

Decisions feel less driven by fear of what might go wrong.

And in that space, something else becomes visible.

Clarity.

Not the kind that comes from having all the answers.

But the kind that comes from no longer needing them all at once.

Because clarity does not come from controlling everything.

It comes from seeing what is already there.

And as trust becomes more natural, something else begins to change quietly.

The weight begins to lift.

Not because life has become easier.

Not because everything is resolved.

But because the need to carry everything so tightly is no longer there.

This is where letting go begins to feel different.

Less like something that is taken away…

and more like something that is released.

Because what created the heaviness was not always the situation itself.

It was the effort to hold it in place.

To control it.

To preserve it.

To make it remain as it once was.

And once that effort is no longer constant, something opens.

Space.

Not emptiness.

But space to move.

Space to think.

Space to experience life without the constant pressure of trying to manage what cannot be managed.

In that space, life begins to feel lighter.

Not perfect.

Not without challenge.

But more fluid.

Because without resistance, movement becomes easier.

Change becomes less threatening.

And what once felt like something to hold onto at all costs…

begins to feel like something that can be appreciated without needing to be controlled.

This is where letting go reveals its true nature.

Not as loss.

But as freedom.

Freedom from the constant effort to make life behave a certain way.

Freedom from the tension of needing things to remain unchanged.

Freedom from the idea that meaning depends on permanence.

Because what is no longer held tightly can finally be experienced differently.

And perhaps that is what people discover when they finally let go.

Not that they have lost something…

but that they have made space for life to move again.

Acceptance is often mistaken for the end of something.

As if it marks a final point.

A conclusion.

A place where everything has been resolved and no further questions remain.

But acceptance rarely feels like an ending.

It feels quieter than that.

Less like a conclusion…

and more like a shift.

A different way of relating to what has already been experienced.

Because acceptance does not remove what has happened.

It does not rewrite the past.

It does not guarantee what will come next.

It simply changes how a person holds all of it.

At first, many people resist acceptance.

Because it can feel like agreeing with what has happened.

Like approving of it.

Like saying that everything unfolded exactly as it should have.

But acceptance is not agreement.

It is understanding.

An acknowledgment of reality as it is…

without needing it to be different.

This distinction is important.

Because people often delay acceptance by believing that it requires them to justify what they have experienced.

But acceptance does not justify.

It recognizes.

It allows something to exist without resistance.

And in that allowance, something else begins to appear.

Peace.

Not the kind that comes from everything being perfect.

But the kind that comes from no longer fighting what cannot be changed.

Because acceptance is what allows that space to remain.

And when acceptance begins to settle, it does not arrive in a dramatic way.

It is not a moment that announces itself.

It appears quietly.

In the absence of resistance.

In the absence of the constant need to revisit what cannot be changed.

In the way certain thoughts no longer carry the same weight they once did.

At first, this shift can be subtle enough to go unnoticed.

A situation that once caused tension no longer feels as immediate.

A memory that once demanded attention now feels softer.

A question that once required an answer no longer feels urgent.

These changes do not happen all at once.

They appear gradually.

And over time, they begin to shape something deeper.

A different relationship with experience itself.

Because acceptance does not remove difficulty.

It changes how difficulty is experienced.

What once felt overwhelming begins to feel manageable.

What once felt confusing begins to feel understandable.

Not because everything has been explained.

But because it no longer needs to be.

This is where acceptance becomes something more than an idea.

It becomes a way of moving through life.

Less reactive.

Less resistant.

More open.

Because when someone no longer needs every moment to make perfect sense…

they begin to experience those moments more fully.

Because peace is not found in certainty.

It is found in understanding without needing certainty.

And as this understanding deepens, something else begins to become clear.

Nothing in life exists separately.

The uncertainty that once felt confusing.

The relationships that revealed hidden parts of the self.

The moments of love that introduced vulnerability.

The experiences of loss that reshaped perspective.

The passage of time that altered what felt important.

The identity that slowly changed through it all.

None of these were isolated.

They were all part of the same movement.

A continuous unfolding.

Each experience influencing the next.

Each realization building upon what came before it.

And when seen together, something begins to make sense.

Not in a way that answers every question.

But in a way that removes the need for every question to be answered.

Because life was never a collection of separate events.

It was always a single experience…

seen from different moments in time.

This is what acceptance reveals.

Not clarity in every detail.

But coherence in the whole.

A recognition that everything that happened…

contributed to the understanding that exists now.

Even the moments that once felt confusing.

Even the experiences that once felt difficult to carry.

They all led here.

Not to a final answer.

But to a different way of seeing.

Because understanding was never about solving life.

It was about seeing it clearly enough to live it.

And in that clarity, something becomes quieter.

The need to search begins to fade.

Not because everything has been found.

But because the search itself is no longer urgent.

Questions may still exist.

But they no longer carry the same weight.

They are no longer something that must be resolved immediately.

They become part of the experience.

Something that can exist without needing to be answered all at once.

This is where life begins to feel different.

Not simpler.

But lighter.

Because the effort to make everything make sense…

is no longer constant.

And without that effort, something else becomes possible.

Presence.

A quiet awareness of what is happening now.

Not as something to analyze.

But as something to experience.

A moment that does not need to lead anywhere.

A conversation that does not need to become something more.

A feeling that does not need to be explained.

Just as it is.

And in that space, something settles.

Not a conclusion.

But a way of being.

A way of moving through life without needing to define it
completely.

Without needing to control it entirely.

Without needing it to always make perfect sense.

Because in that space, life is no longer something to hold onto.

It is something to be experienced.

Eventually people begin to notice something unexpected.

Life never fully explains itself.

Not completely.

Not in the way people once hoped it would.

There is no final moment where everything suddenly becomes
clear.

No point where every decision finally reveals its perfect meaning.

No place where uncertainty disappears forever.

For a long time this realization feels frustrating.

People want answers.

They want explanations.

They want the reassurance that all the effort was leading somewhere precise.

But the longer someone observes life, the more something else begins to appear.

Understanding.

Not the kind that solves everything.

The kind that allows things to exist without needing to be solved.

Because life was never really a puzzle.

It only looked like one from a distance.

Up close it is something else entirely.

An experience.

A landscape.

A long series of moments that slowly shape the person living through them.

Some moments joyful.

Some confusing.

Some difficult enough to change a person forever.

But all of them part of the same quiet unfolding.

And somewhere along the way most people begin to notice something simple.

The search was never about finding the perfect answer.

It was about learning how to live with the questions.

That is usually the moment life begins to feel lighter.

Not because everything suddenly makes sense.

But because it no longer has to.

And perhaps that is where everything eventually arrives.

Not at an answer.

But at an understanding.

That life was never something that needed to be solved.

Not something that required perfect clarity.

Not something that followed a single, predictable path.

It was always something else.

Something to move through.

Something to experience.

Something to learn from...

without needing to fully define it.

Because every moment that once felt uncertain...

every relationship that revealed something unexpected...

every loss that changed perspective...

every passing year that reshaped what mattered...

every version of the self that evolved along the way...

None of it was separate.

It was all part of the same unfolding.

And once that becomes clear, something shifts.

The need for certainty fades.

The pressure to understand everything disappears.

The weight of trying to control what cannot be controlled begins to
lift.

And in its place, something quieter remains.

Not an answer.

Not a conclusion.

Just a clear awareness.

That life was never asking to be solved.
Only to be understood.

www.ingramcontent.com/pod-product-compliance
Lightning Source LLC
Chambersburg PA
CBHW051443050726
47593CB00005B/1914